WHITE CANE FISHING:

FORTY YEARS OF HILARIOUS ADVENTURES OF A BLIND ANGLER

Daniel C. Rogers

D1521703

Dedicated to Douglas Arthur Flantz

(Written and typed by the author in 2022-23 on my talking computer)

TABLE OF CONTENTS

PROLOGUE

When I was a senior at Winona State College in 1974, I learned that I would gradually lose my eyesight to an inherited, (I have three blind brothers), retinal defect which is progressive. I struggled with this for a while and even feared for my sanity after total loss of vision later. After much soul searching, I finally made my conviction. I promised myself I would never let my eventual blindness stand in the way of what I want to do with my life, either professionally or in my personal life including my hobbies and eventual happy addiction of fishing.

It has always been a tremendous challenge but I have been able to keep my conviction I made with myself, for the most part. I consider myself fortunate and grateful that I got my college education finished before my vision really began fading. With some help and perseverance, I even managed to have a successful professional career for 38 years although I was blind nearly the entire time.

It all started in 1981 when I met Doug who eventually married my kid sister. He and I are still putting up with each other in the boat. Sometimes we call ourselves "dumb and dumber." One resort owner named Dr. Anita called us Mutt & Jeff. We play off each other in a comical way to this day. The following is the story of countless fishing adventures with him and many other anglers all over Minnesota, North Dakota Ontario, and Manitoba. Although the stories are factual there might be "occasional embellishment" common to anglers. I hope you enjoy them as much as I delighted in writing them for you.

Parenthetically, my fishing hobby/addiction is not just about catching fish which is still a childish thrill for me. It's also about male bonding and being on the water in the great outdoors which is exciting theatre in itself.

It is not my intention to educate you about how to catch fish. I assume nearly all of you already know how to put those slimy critters in your live well, bucket or creel. Therefore, I am only including stories that are comical, poignant, unusual, or terrifying. Believe it or not, I have fished hundreds of times that were uneventful but they are not much fun to write about. Of course, I won't tell you about all the times we got skunked.

WE NEVER GIVE UP IN THE FACE OF ADVERSITY SINCE IT IS CRITICAL TO OUR MENTAL HEALTH THAT WE HAVE LOTS OF FUN IN LIFE.

Chapter One: Fishing the 1980'S

For Doug and I, our first fishing adventure took place in June of 1981. We had a cabin on Leech Lake in Minnesota. We dragged our wives along, kicking and screaming. They were good friends although they would not get into the boat, which we didn't mind too terribly much. On our first day we hired an ancient guide named Howard. We only caught nine walleyes all day which Howard said was the fewest he ever caught. We grinned about that fishing lie.

The next day we noticed most of the boats were drifting off the east side of Bear Island. We started drifting the same area but caught nothing although the anglers all around us were catching walleyes left and right. We finally, asked a fisherman what they were using for bait, and he said shiner minnows. We were using only fathead minnows. We went back to the resort and bought shiner minnows. It turned out that the shiners were spawning in that area and the walleyes were clustered there to gorge on them. We caught two limits of fish in the rain. We had never heard of this before, but we learned from it. Our wives survived the week without too much wear and tear!

Our first Canadian fishing trip was a wild one in 1982. Doug, myself and my brother Mark drove to Bright Sand Lake in Ontario, which isn't by anything. We drove all night in dense fog. In fact, the fog was so bad on the north shore of Lake Superior we had to send Mark outside to find the road, and when we finally got to the Graham Road by the little village of Ignace, we thought we died and went to hell. That road was like a washboard and we could not go faster than 15 miles per hour, usually less. To make matters worse, the sunroof of Doug's Grand Prix had some bad leak, so we had to wear our rain suits in the car due to heavy rain which really sucked! All the while we were fighting to stay awake after driving all night. It was Mark's job to keep Doug awake while driving but Mark fell asleep right away.

Although Doug had been fishing in Ontario many times since age nine, he was never on Bright Sand Lake, so we didn't really know the roads to take. We took a wrong turn onto an actual logging road. There were big trees down all around us as well as waist high boulders. It looked like the sort of place where dinosaurs might hang out. We got out of the car several times to remove debris from the barely discernible road. Doug finally stopped the car and ran up a hill to find a lake. He was gone so long we decided a bear must have got him. When he finally returned, we had to unhook the boat from his car to turn around since we were definitely on the wrong route.

At last, we got back to the Graham road and to our correct turn off to the public access. The access had no dock and was very shallow. We loaded everything into our little borrowed 14-foot boat and had to walk it out to deeper water. Ever had to portage a 14-foot aluminum boat with a 10-horsepower motor? We did to get to Bright Sand. To make matters worse there were huge boulders we had to climb over with the boat, motor, gas cans, tent, sleeping bags and coolers of food. We also carted in three cases of ale in bottles. After that we always brought canned beer. Whew!

The fishing was great as was the unspoiled wilderness. Believe it or not, when we finally got the boat up the rapids into Bright Sand Lake Doug ran into his Little League coach on the water! We did not know he would be there. What are the odds?

On our first full day of fishing Mark was struggling. He kept messing up his reel, getting snagged and missing fish after fish. Finally, in exasperation, he threw his rod down in the boat and yelled, "I don't know how to fish.! I felt sorry for him and after a couple of minutes of silence I said, "Mark, it's okay if you don't know how to fish. There is no better place to learn how than Canada. Doug will teach you how, won't you Doug?" Doug quipped, "Sure. I would love to." After an hour of instruction Mark got the hang of it and started boating walleyes. In fact, he was so happy he put a saucepan on his head and fished all afternoon like that. Not sure why we had a saucepan in the boat, but it drew odd stares from the little league coach's boat! I was very pleased to see my baby brother happier.

Bright Sand Lake was supposedly known for a large population of giant pike, but we never located them. We caught lots of walleyes and I got the biggest one but it only weighed five pounds.

One quiet night while sitting around the campfire we started hearing the strangest noises out on the water. We walked down to the water and witnessed millions of minnows jumping out of the water all across the small lake over and over again. We had never seen anything like this before so we watched it for a long time. We brainstormed about what could cause such a strange phenomenon but never knew with certainty. Maybe it had something to do with the barometer but if that was the case then bigger fish should have been jumping too. We could only guess that the lake had been invaded by a big school of marauding predator fish or Nessie herself and the minnows were trying to escape! It was nothing short of spectacular and a bit eerie. We have been on the water hundreds of times since then and never observed such a natural event again.

Unfortunately, Doug was responsible for bringing the food and did not bring enough so we lost weight on this trip. He said we did not come here to eat but to fish! Since then, I have always happily taken the responsibility to bring all our food and, of course, now we gain weight. However, we never went back to Bright Sand Lake.

The next year, 1983, Doug and I as well as my brother Mark went to the English River by Kenora, Ontario. We drove all night with Doug's dads' boat, a leaky Lund with a 25 hp motor and 6 horse kicker. We got to Gosh Hawk landing just before dawn. Since this access is on the First Nation White Dog Reserve, we woke up a Native guy who was sleeping in a little shack on the side of an old gravel road. We only had to pay $20. To launch but he said there was a bear at the garbage dump by the dock. We drove down to the access and decided to wait until daybreak even though we could not spot a black bear anywhere, to our relief.

When we finally loaded up our gear and food, we noticed there was some wind. We got across Gosh Hawk Lake easily but then had to cross a large lake called One Man Lake. It was choppy but we tried it anyway. Mark and I were not smart enough to wear our rainsuits and got soaked with splash from the waves. Plus, it was a cool morning. By the time we finally got to the hilltop island campsite we felt frozen and could not stop shivering. Doug was dry since he was driving in the back of the tiller boat. Mark and I took off all our wet clothes and climbed in our sleeping bags to recoup our body heat. By the time we finally warmed up Doug had carried all our heavy gear up the hill by himself. Mark and I laughed about this and later told him we were faking our hypothermia just so he had to do all the work. His reply was very naughty and physically impossible.

The English River in that area of northwest Ontario is on a Chippewa Reserve so we always paid them to camp on their land and fish their productive waters. It is a chain of lakes and very primitive. There are no campsites so we made our own. There were no amenities and our bathroom was often a 2X4 nailed horizontally between two birch trees. Sometimes our toilet was just hanging our butts over a fallen tree at which time we always prayed out loud there were no wood ticks on the log! Sadly, a couple of times those prayers went unanswered. Yikes!

We fished the English River for four days until most of our ice melted. This was before 5 Day coolers were invented. That water system is littered with stumps so we got hundreds of snags and break offs. One day Doug had 19 break offs and ran out of swivel snaps so we had to tease him about it. Nineteen is still the record and nearly his only claim to fame! LOL

We went to a bay which was named Scarrow's Bay. It was named after Doug's family friend who only had one hand. Kenny Scarrow preferred to fish alone. He always came in at the end of the day with more big fish than anyone and no one could figure out how he netted fish and held his rod at the same time since he only had one hand. For several days he would not reveal his location. When he finally did, they decided to name it Scarrow's Bay. For many years we caught lots of big fish in that bay especially in front of the beaver lodge. It has since become the stuff of legend and I considered it nearly magical; the epitome of fishing mystique.

In 1983 Mark, Doug and I went back to the English River for four more days of fishing nirvana. This time we had the good fortune of camping on what we call Big Point. The first morning Mark was too tired to go out so we left him in the tent. While on Scarrow's Bay we ran out of minnows. Doug found a fathead minnow lying in a small puddle of gas on the bottom of the boat. He put it on his purple Fuzz-E-Grub jib and hooked a big one! It was a long fight and stayed straight down so we knew it was a walleye. I still had some eyesight at that point so I grabbed the net intending to scoop up the brute. When Doug finally got it to the surface, I made a poorly aimed lunge at it. When I lifted the net out of the water, I could feel that the fish was hanging on the left side of the net hoop. I jerked the net to the left as Doug was nervously barking out orders. It tumbled into the net and we got it in the boat. We weighed it on three different De-Liars and chose the one that indicated the beast weighed 8.5 pounds on the nose. We had to celebrate so we mixed up some swill in the boat. We poured brandy into a big 7up bottle that was nearly empty and warm. It wasn't long until we were well on the way, both with a party buzz and the long drive back to camp.

There were floating logs all through the system so with the motor wide open Doug slalomed the boat while I was hanging on for dear life. We were shouting with joy all the way. It was a hair-raising ride and when we got close to Big Point we started yelling, "trophy, trophy!" Doug rammed the rock island at full speed and we both took a little flight. I ended up hanging over the point of the boat hoping I had not lost the family jewels!

My brother Mark ran out of the tent in his underwear to see what the ruckus was about. When we showed him our catch, he was mighty impressed but then cursed himself for staying in the tent. He missed the big show, so we called him a wuss! Doug took that fish home and it still hangs on his wall. Somehow it grew to nine pounds even over the years.

On that trip Doug brought a very ugly rubber mask that covered his entire head. It was like a Halloween mask that made him look like a gruesome, deformed monster with a bald head with ridges! Anytime a boat got anywhere near us he put it on. He drew a lot of stares that week but it had the desired effect of keeping the other boats away! It was also fun.

In 1983 I went back to the English River with Doug, my brother Bill and his 13-year-old son, Chad. Four people in a 16-foot boat was too much but we made it work out of desperation. We camped on Big Point again in my tent. On a full moon night about midnight, we heard an outboard motor just as we were drifting into slumber, or in some cases passing out. The stranger boat pulled onto our island. We were a bit apprehensive since we did not know if they were armed. We had a shotgun in the tent but certainly did not want to use it. Two Indian fishing guides from the resort far down the system came to our tent offering money for alcohol. We told them we had none to spare, but they persisted. We could soon tell that they would not leave until we sold them some beer and for all we knew they might have a gun. We were scared. We finally sold them a 12 pack for $20. American and they left. However, as they walked away, we could hear them rattling some bushes right in front of our tent. We then heard the clink of bottles. They had stashed liquor in those bushes, and we never knew it. After driving out onto the lake they shut off their motor to party. We never saw them again for which we were very grateful even though they were not nasty.

One day our group was fishing a massive log jam for pike while a black thunder cloud approached slowly. It took about two hours for the cloud to catch us and it was a pike jamboree until then. The closer the blackness came the crazier the pike were. They savagely attacked every spoon and plug we threw right up to the log jam. There must have been a thousand of them in there. We hooked a pike on every cast and a few were bigger. It was great fun until the blackness got above us. Then we got off the water for an hour. When we went back there, we could hardly scare up a fish.

One day Chad was getting on our nerves since he was such a squirrely kid, so we dropped him off on a small island at his request and we were happy to oblige him. He casted all around the island for an hour but no fish. We kept him in sight the whole time and it was a nice break for all concerned. Ever since then we have called it Chad's island.

As soon as we picked him up, we noticed a loon nesting with loon chicks in the grass on the other side of the narrow island. Right then, a bald eagle landed in the tree top right above the loons. The mother loon went nuts, squawking loudly in protest. She knew the chicks were in danger of the eagle making a quick

snack of them. We had never seen anything like this before and stopped fishing to observe the waterfowl theatre unfolding before our very eyes. This captivating scenario dragged on for twenty minutes before the eagle, for whatever reason, gave up and flew away. The hen finally settled down and we were a bit relieved there was no massacre. We caught no more fish in that area the rest of the afternoon.

One afternoon when we were filleting our catch by our campsite a boat pulled up to visit us. Three local Natives got out to talk to us. The father, mother and little boy were very friendly and just wanted to exchange fishing information. He was a guide and told us about a long grassy bar right alongside our island about half a mile out. We did not know about this but it was very productive especially for smallmouth bass. His boss' name was Sharon so he smiled and said he named that spot Sharon's Hole! Honest! By the way, the little boy pooped on our island which we thought was pretty cute. Perhaps that was the main reason they stopped there. We fished Sharon's Hole many times and had good luck on walleyes and big smallmouth bass.

The day before we left the game warden from the Ontario Ministry of Natural Resources came to our island when we were frying fish for shore lunch. They checked our licenses and told us that starting the next year we cannot camp here again on Big Point. When we asked why they said the resort that was miles down the system did not want outbackers, as they called us, because they were advertising themselves as a fly-in resort only and seeing us camping made them look dishonest, which they were indeed. The officials told us we cannot camp beyond Burnt Off island from now on. We were very bummed out about this, but we vowed that they would not chase us out of the English River ever. We were also disappointed the MNR assisted that resort in the lie of false advertising.

The day we were to leave it was windy and the waves on One Man Lake were big; too big to venture out in our little 16-foot craft. We waited most of the day and were nearly out of food. Finally, about supper time we decided to make a run for it. When we got to One Man the waves were frightening so we only went a little way before heading for shore. We found a small island and drove into the quiet water between it and the mainland. Unlike the rest of the English River the water in that little channel was gin clear. We found a place to pitch our tent but had to slide down a little hill into the tent.

We pitched our tent close to a big pile of animal feces. We could not decide if it was bear scat or moose crap or wolf dung but it made us a little nervous since this is how predators mark their territory. It was a restless night but we had no visitors. Yippee!

At dawn we heard an outboard motor down the lake. We got excited and even inspired. We figured if they can do it so can we. We hastily packed up and took off for Gosh Hawk landing. We made it across the gigantic One Man Lake at a slow pace. When we saw the dock, we cheered with joy and relief. By the time we got the boat and gear loaded into my big Ford van and finally got to Kenora, we were famished from no supper the night before and no breakfast that morning. We spent massive amounts of money at McDonalds in Kenora. It was a fitting end to another great and wild trip. As always, we left Ontario with limits of walleyes which was six back then.

During the 1980's we made several more trips to the legendary English River; sometimes twice in one summer. We camped on cemetery island at the far end of One Man Lake. We called it this since the local Chippewa people had an actual cemetery with many white crosses on one side of the island and the other side was clear and grassy, good for camping. There was even a large concrete retaining wall on the west side of that island to protect the grave from being washed out into the lake from big waves! The Chippewa people said we could camp on the grassy side as long as we did not disturb their graves. Interestingly, they said they would not camp or live there due to spirits, but they were okay with us being there. We suspected they thought we were foolish for doing so but we did not care.

After a few trips that beloved system started feeling like home to me but Doug was fishing there since he was nine years old. In fact, when he was ten years old, he claims he saw a large Nessie-like serpent with its head and three humps and a tail above the water, many feet apart. He still claims it was about sixty feet long! It was grayish brown and had a snake-like head. Unfortunately, no one else in his boat saw it as they were looking the other way so there was skepticism. He tried to yell "sea monster," but he could not get the word out in time since he was awe struck. We have asked him to tell this story many times and it never changes. This sighting was on One Man Lake which is over 200 feet deep. No one else in our parties or others have had such a sighting but we all loved the idea of an ancient serpent lurking in the depths of that remote lake.

In 1986, we struck out on our one and only fishing trip to Manitoba. I went with two brothers, Bill and Mark, as well as Bill's son Chad and, of course, Doug. We stacked a fourteen-foot boat on top of a sixteen-footer with wooden brackets made just for this purpose. Then we tied it down for added insurance. The five of us piled into a big Dodge Ram van and tooled up I 29 to Winnipeg. When gassing up in Winnipeg a car leaving the gas station had a guy yelling out his window at us: "go home Americans! We don't want you here! Go home!" He yelled this angrily several times. We were shocked and did not feel welcome in Winnipeg and this put a damper on our trip.

Furthermore, on the way to Canada we discovered we forgot to bring two landing nets, one for each boat. While gassing up there was another fisherman there so we pretty much begged him to sell us his net. He grudgingly agreed and we gave him $20. American for the small net and thanked him profusely. We were happy to leave Winnipeg.

We got to Lake Manigotogan in White Shell Provincial Park just after dawn. We used a resort boat access and filled our water jugs from the camp pump. We should have asked permission for this but we could not find anyone around. As we were about to load the two big water jugs into the boats the resort owner drove up on a three-wheeler, grabbed our water jugs and began emptying them out on the ground, the whole time yelling at us. "I know my government says I have to let you use my dock but that does not mean I have to let you use my water!" Then he sped off. We felt terrible. We managed to salvage half the water before it all drained out. To make matters even more humiliating, four out of five of us needed to buy fishing licenses from that guy. We waited for a while, hoping he would cool off. Then we went to the resort office and apologized. Surprisingly, he apologized for blowing up and sold us the licenses.

As we were loading our gear into our boats, we saw a guy go out in an inner tube with a little paddle in one hand and a rod in the other. We had never seen this before or even heard of it so we drew a sweeping generalization that Manitobans are an odd lot, indeed.

On this trip I brought plywood, 2X4's, a hammer and nails and built a cooking table and fish cleaning table otherwise we would have been cooking in the dirt. They worked well and we left them for the next "out backers."

Another low light was one rainy morning I had to crap in the woods in the rain. The rest of the day I had damp undies but there was no other option. This we called roughing it.

One of the highlights of this trip occurred one evening at dusk. We were all in our tents but just before dark Doug got up to pee. While wearing only his underwear. This turned out to be a mistake since the mosquitos were ferocious. To cope with this his strategy was to keep moving. While we peered out the screen windows of the tents, we witnessed Doug running back and forth sideways while peeing at the same time! It was a hilarious spectacle and we laughed our butts off. Lucky for us, he had his back to us the whole time.

We did not feel welcome in Manitoba but managed to catch a lot of walleyes below a small waterfall that saved our trip. We never ventured into Manitoba again.

In the mid 1980's Doug, Ross and I went to George & Sophie's Resort near Outing, Minnesota. It was the walleye opener and we fished Lake Emily. There was a stream connecting that lake to Lake Mary. We started backtrolling in the narrow stream in a tight circle and were putting fish on our stringer. Another boat pulled up close to us with one occupant wearing an orange slicker. He asked if we got our stringer of fish on the spot we were on. Doug fibbed and said no we got them on the main lake. Suddenly, Doug yelled, "hey you look like Al Lindner!" The guy replied, "I am Al Lindner." As he drove off Doug yelled, "Good bye, Al Lindner!" That was the day we out-fished the legendary Al Lindner of TV fishing fame. We laughed about this all weekend and boasted about it for years. We loved the idea that we had to tell him where to catch fish.

The next day we got a hot tip at a bait shop about Rabbit Lake which was new to us but nearby. We found the lake and were pleased there were few boats around. It was a hot, sunny day. We anchored in 8 feet of water and began catching nice panfish. It was a quiet day with no wind and I heard no other boats around. When I had to pee, I went right over the side into the lake. The guys cursed at me since I pulled it out right in front of a cute woman in a pink bikini! I had no idea there was another boat nearby. Doug yelled to her and the guy in their boat that I am blind. I yelled that I am sorry. I felt very sheepish that I publicly humiliated myself once again due to my blindness. I am getting very good at that. Ross and Doug still tease me about that incident. I was very grateful her boyfriend/husband did not pull out a gun and shoot me or cast a big Daredevil at my head, the latter of which is the secret fear of all anglers!

By the way, George, as noted above, grew up in the great depression and had very hard times. He had lost money in bank failures. His solution and a type of insurance was to stuff mason jars with wads of cash and bury them in the woods upon which his resort rested. He also stashed some under the floor boards of his cabin which were later found. However, since he never told his wife or anyone else exactly where he buried those jars they are still there somewhere. He never made a map either since he did not want anyone to find it. Doug and I have occasionally toyed with the idea of digging up his property to find the jars but we would not know where to start. Besides, after George and Sophie died the resort changed hands.

In the summer of 1988, Doug, my 13-year-old nephew Christopher, and I went to fish the Winnipeg River just outside of Minaki, Ontario by Kenora. We were tenting again and had a map. We found an abandoned island to camp on. The map said it was called Dead Man's Island which we hoped was not a harbinger of things to come! We never fished this system before but it had the same stained water as the English River so we were able to catch walleyes on bright, sunny afternoons. We suspected the two river systems were connected somewhere.

One night a howling gale came up and picked up with a driving rain. My tent leaked and I woke up with a soggy sleeping bag. After daybreak, Doug got up to make coffee on the Coleman stove and to check on his dad's leaky Lund boat. He did not come back for a long time, so Christopher decided to go check on Doug. Christopher did not return either, so I was getting concerned. Then I finally hauled my carcass out of the tent and the guys were nowhere to be found. My eyesight by then was poor so I could not find the trail down to the shore which was a large rock ledge. I yelled for them and Christopher came to fetch me. It turned out that the heavy wind smashed the boat up against to rock ledge all night, puncturing the hull right on the seam near the back of the boat. When Doug first saw the boat the back half was submerged and half the boat was full of water. He started bailing it out with a five-gallon bucket but made little headway. When he spotted the bubbles coming up by the hole, he realized why he struggled to lower the water level. We pulled the boat sideways onto the ledge so the puncture was now out of the water. With more bailing we got most of the water out even though there was no bilge pump. If it weren't for the fact that we knew Doug's brother-in-law was on the same system with two boats we would have been very frightened that we might never get off Dead Mans Island due to a boat that was marginally seaworthy.

They showed up that afternoon for a shore lunch which we planned ahead of time. Walter had some of that 2-stage bonging glue and patched the hole. He said it would take hours to dry but the waves were so high we did not want to venture out anyway. The other two boats were bigger. We topped the glued hole with duct tape. That night my sleeping bag was still damp including on the inside so I slept in a large lawn & leaf bag in my sleeping bag as a liner. It worked! This was not the first time I did this on a fishing trip. We fished the next two days and only had to bail out the boat every couple of hours with a small scoop made for this purpose.

One day we were trolling by an island when Doug spotted a very strange thing. The island was a hill and there was a white rivulet of water flowing down the hill into the lake. We could not figure this one out and our curiosity got the best of us so we went to shore and tied the boat to a tree. When we got to the top of the hill, we were amazed to find a jet of white water shooting out of the ground! It was only a one-foot geyser but continuous rather than intermittent like Old Faithful. I cupped the water in my hands and smelled it. It smelled just like any water, so I stuck my tongue in it, and it also tasted just like water; no sulfur or chemical odor or taste at all.

I don't know much about geology, but we surmised there must be a limestone deposit underground that tainted the water. We guessed that the water weight from high water level forced that white water to fountain upwards, but we were not certain. We had never seen anything like this before and not since either.

Fishing on the Winnipeg River was great, especially along the "clay banks" but we did not catch any lunkers. Our biggest walleye was 6.5 pounds which I caught on Christopher's rod. We never returned to the Winnipeg River. Too many bad memories, I guess.

In 1989 we decided to try a different lake; one that was new for us. Basket Lake Camp is north of Dryden, Ontario and run by the

Olga North family. It's the only resort on the small lake so there were few boats. This trip it was Doug, his childhood friend Ross and Ross's cousin Virgil as well as myself. We went in the same old leaky Lund boat, a sixteen-footer which was crowded for four anglers.

This was the first time on this water so we didn't know where to fish. The fishing was good but the practical jokes rivaled the fishing. Ross was always full of mischief. For instance, one morning Ross ran back up to the tent to get something while we waited in the boat. His tent had an attached screen house, and he found a live bird in it. Most people would have chased it out but not ross. The first thing that popped into his deranged mind was, "what can I do with this bird?" He grabbed the bird and stuffed it in his jacket pocket. When he got to his boat seat, he was sitting right in front of Doug who was at the tiller helm. Doug was looking to the back so ross held the bird inches from the back of Doug's head and said, "hey, Dougie, look at this." When Doug turned around the bird was two inches from his nose, and he yelled and jumped. Ross released the bird alive and we all had a good laugh. There were other practical jokes but they are too disgusting and naughty to share.

Virgil was a problem on this trip. He only did three things all week: smoked cigarettes nonstop, talk nonstop and drink sugar Cokes nonstop. He did no work at all and did not help out with anything even though he had good vision. After a couple of days, I felt like leaving him on an island like the pirates used to do with trouble makers.

Alas, as of this writing, poor Virgil recently perished from lung cancer due to chain smoking. In his last years he became an extreme hoarder. When Ross and his wife inherited Virgil's home, they had a terrible time with clean up. There were dozens of large garbage bags of pop cans cluttering the house as well as a full-sized grizzly bear mount standing up. After weeks of cleaning and filling many dumpsters, they finally found someone to haul away the giant bear which Virgil killed in Alaska. They also found several large checks that he never bothered to cash. None of us had any idea he had become a hoarder and neither did his neighbors. May he rest in peace, anyway.

We did not boat any huge fish on this voyage to Basket Lake but ate lots of walleyes and brought some home. We ended up falling in love with Basket Lake and returned there many times. It is a very special getaway.

CHAPTER TWO: ICE FISHING THE 1980's

Lake Mille Lacs is a large, shallow walleye factory in central Minnesota. In its heyday it was probably the best walleye lake in the country. One of our fishing traditions was to rent an ice house on Mille Lacs every New Years weekend which we did many times starting in the 80's. This big lake had two lane plowed roads and even streets signs on the ice! On any given weekend there might be a thousand people living on the ice.

New Years Eve on Mille Lacs was always wild and exciting. People would shoot Roman candles off the top of their fish houses and nearly everyone was partying. We never did find a sober person there on New Years Eve which certainly upheld the drinking reputation of ice anglers. We always heard rumors of prostitutes on snowmobiles on Mille Lacs but never encountered any.

Back then I could still see good enough to play poker with my jumbo index playing cards. Ice fishing was often slow so we did a lot of quarter ante poker. One New Years Eve we were playing five card stud and drinking beer until the cows came home. Sometime before midnight there was a knock on our door. We yelled, "come in!" Two burly guys walked in without even introducing themselves and proudly exclaimed, "we are hog farmers from Marshall, and we are high on cocaine!" They had sold a load of hogs and spent some of the profits on cocaine.

They were very high and did not seem to know what they were doing so we just humored them. Somehow, they noticed we were playing poker and one of them asked if he could play. We said yes so Doug and I and the miscreant sat to deal. The guy was so high it impaired his judgement or else he knew nothing about poker. He ended up betting $20. On a pair of deuces and lost. Altogether, he gambled away nearly $100. But he did not seem to care. They left happily intoxicated. A little while later we noticed the line from our rattle reel next to the door was going out the door. We went out and followed the line to the next house. When we went inside and discovered the hook was stuck in the pants of the guy who lost money to us and was now passed out on his bunk. We unhooked the line and left without waking him. Honest!

We usually stayed two nights in our shack and that second night we were again playing cards after a nice fish fry when there was another knock at our door. We yelled, "who is it?" A woman shouted, "is my 14-year-old daughter in there?" Since we were a little drunk, we decided to have some fun with her, so we replied, "yes!" She stormed in with an angry scowl on her face. It did not take long for her to see that the wayward girl was not afoot, and the mom stomped out. We wondered what next? We never knew if she found the teenager.

Another New Year's Eve contained similar alcohol adventures on Lake Mille Lacs. Our rental house had a heater that was too big. Although we were wearing short sleeves, we still had to turn down the heat. That night we must have turned it down too much causing the pilot light to go out. We had never seen a stove like this and did not know how to relight it. Doug and I drove off the ice to the resort renter. The fish house technician was even drunker than us but the owner told him he had to go with us to help with our heater. We tossed him in the back seat of my station wagon and drove to our house which involved driving very slowly over a homemade bridge over a big ice heave which was a common sight on Mille Lacs. When we finally got to our ice house we had to wake up the guy in the back seat. Somehow, he managed to light our stove without blowing us up for which we were grateful. He noticed we had a spare bunk and asked if he could sleep there. We politely demurred and he went to the nearest house and slept with some friends of his. It was after midnight, so we finally retired.

Once on New Years weekend on that same lake, we had a blizzard that dumped 17 inches of snow on the ice. Fortunately, we had a shovel to clear out the car and the resort plow truck plowed us out.

Oh, yes, sometimes we even caught fish on Mille Lacs. Rattle reels worked best and required less work than jigging an ice rod. If the walleyes weren't biting, sometimes a giant school of jumbo perch were below our shack, and we would catch dozens on small fatheads on both rods and rattle reels. We kept many and fried up a mess of them which were just as tasty as walleyes. Occasionally, we would hook a big eelpout which is a prehistoric fish that looks like a fat eel. They fought harder than walleyes but we did not fillet out any for consumption. Although some call them "poor man's lobster," we thought they were so ugly we never could bring ourselves to eat one. They bit best on jigs. Eelpout are also known as burbot and are only active in the winter and usually dormant in the summer. They are blackish. When we held them to dislodge the hook they wrapped around our arm like an eel.

On yet another Mille Lacs ice trip I actually drove my van while out on the ice at night. Doug was in the van with me to guide me along the two-lane road. A car came from the other direction but I could only see the headlights a little. I said to Doug, "don't you think that driver would crap if he knew a blind man was at the wheel of this van?" We laughed and, amazingly, I only ran into one snowbank before Doug took the wheel. It was a great thrill for me which I did not repeat!

In the 1980's my brother-in-law Doug and I started ice fishing Lake Minnewashka in Glenwood and Starbuck Minnesota. This lake is the thirteenth largest in the state and was known for excellent walleye fishing in December. The ice was usually not thick enough to drive on in that month, so we usually stacked our houses and gear on snow sleds and walked out about a half mile from shore and a half mile laterally from the legendary Glenwood Ballroom where Garrison Keeler once performed his radio show Prairie Home Companion. However, we were not there for that.

Our houses were homemade and folded up like a large suitcase. The floor and both ends were wood and the rest was heavy canvas. These houses were only 6 feet long so barely had room for our cots. We had home-made heaters we bought from a guy in Madison, Minnesota who made them. They burned so clean we did not need a chimney although our shacks had a chimney hole built in.

The first time I ice fished Minnewaska there was a 49 below windchill so we thought we would not catch much. However, we caught walleyes all night on minnows and rattle reels.

Unfortunately, we made the mistake of setting up our houses too close to each other so when we had a walleye that took out a lot of line it got wrapped around the line in the other guy's house. What a mess!

We always brought a bread sack full of sandwiches wrapped in foil so our breakfast and lunch was hot food we heated up on our heater, which had a flat top. Doug always made coffee for us on his Coleman stove. For supper he usually fried up cheese burgers.

One night I had just fallen asleep when I thought I heard my rattle reel rattling. I decided I must be dreaming and I ignored it. Then I dreamed the zipper door on the front of my fish house was being unzipped and someone pulled in a fish and threw it on the ice and then baited my hook and dropped it back down my hole and then zipped up my tent.

The next morning when I was standing in front of my house getting some fresh air the guy next door came over to tell me he was walking past my house the night before and heard the rattle so he pulled in the fish for me. We laughed and I thanked him. I even offered to give him the 2-pound walleye but he refused. It turned out to be the same guy who had the two story ice house that slanted like the Leaning Tower of Pisa! He was always getting ticketed for too many lines in the water but he kept doing it anyway.

There is a special camaraderie among anglers and we nearly always help each other including stopping to help change a flat tire on a boat trailer of which we had many.

CHAPTER THREE: FISHING THE 1990'S / BREAKING IN TYLER

In 1992, Doug and my sister, who were married, adopted a one-month-old boy. Doug and I desperately wanted him to be a fisherman so we devised a plan which he hoped would do the trick. Doug had a nine-pound walleye on his wall from the English River as noted above. I asked him to hold the baby boy, Tyler, up to that fish on the wall and say the word "fish, fish, fish" over and over again. He did this nearly every day for over a year. Furthermore, for Tyler's first birthday I gave him a Mickey Mouse tackle box. He immediately began sucking on Mickey's big ears which comprised the handle.

In the summer of 1991, five of us went to Lake of the Woods with two boats. Ross's brother owned land on Oak Island so we pitched our tents there. The island was the summer home for thousands of orioles. They had the long nests and beautiful birdsong which we enjoyed all week. The bay in front of Sunset Lodge, which had a great restaurant, was productive but calamity was just around the corner.

A typhoon came up that night. We estimated the howling wind was probably at least 40 mph, maybe 50. When we got up that morning, we saw that Virgil's old, fiberglass boat was swamped in the middle of the bay! When we got to the dock, we noticed his tie ropes were hanging limp on the dock with the anvil cleats from his boat still attached. They were both hanging loose. At that point I was very grateful I tied my boat with heavy dock line to the built-in rings on the front and back of my boat since they held.

We climbed into my boat and dropped Ross and Virgil off at the half-sunk boat with big buckets for bailing. After a lot of heavy bailing, they got the back end up on the surface. We were amazed his motor started but his bilge pump failed so still had a lot of water under the false bottom. Virgil drove to the public access and headed his vehicle to Warroad to buy a new pump. Later that day he finally got all the water out of his boat.

Unfortunately, the typhoon continued all that day and night so we could only fish a small protected area. The next morning Virgil's boat was swamped in the bay again. At this point it was no longer comical. Since the wind never did subside much, we packed up and went home a day early with our tails between our legs again. However, at least we had a couple of great fish fries and yet another wacky adventure as well as some campfire parties. Sometimes I serenaded the guys with my harmonica around the campfire and they always pretended they hated it. Perhaps they really did.

In the early 1990's Doug, my brother Bill and I ventured to Voyagers National Park which borders Ontario and is Minnesota's only National Park. We tried to rent a campsite on an island of Lake Kabetogama but they were all occupied. We had to settle for one on the mainland. It was the nicest campsite we ever found, with two tent pads and a steel bin for our coolers that was guaranteed bear proof and our own little lagoon for tying up my boat. Although it came with a picnic table and firepit there was no dock. The privy was a wooden toilet down the trail in the woods. It was not an outhouse, just a free-standing wooden toilet wide open. While there every morning we wondered if a bear would saunter right up to us but that never happened. We theorized that the odor kept them at bay, luckily. Nevertheless, it was a bit eerie.

Since it was August the walleye fishing was slow, especially since we did not know where to fish. This was our first trip to this huge lake. However, one hot afternoon we witnessed a very cute natural spectacle. There was a large flat rock ledge on shore that sloped down to the water. A family of lake otters, including three babies were sliding down the rock on their bellies over and over again. It was fun to watch them play so we stayed for quite a while. We did not know otters could play.

We managed to catch enough fish for supper that night. Unfortunately, Doug made the dumb mistake of dumping the fishy grease out of the frying pan into the dirt close to our picnic table. Big mistake!

That night in our tent we were just drifting off to sleep when we heard a loud banging noise close by that scared the crap out of us! Bill looked out the tent screen window and saw a large black bear standing on its hind legs! It was pounding on our steel bin where we put our coolers of food. Then with one paw it backhanded my Coleman lantern off the bin, and it went flying. It landed with a loud crash that frightened the bruin but only for a second or two. The guys saw another bear too. One of them came over to the picnic table and found the fish grease and started licking up the dirt that was soaked with it. Then the brute ambled over to our tent. It came right up to the screen window on Doug's end of the tent. We were scared shitless! I was shaking since I could hear it sniffing and snorting, apparently trying to determine if we were edible. Doug was literally inches from the bear and I could hear him hyperventilating and I was shaking with fear! We had no weapon but my folding buck knife. Our axe was outside, unfortunately. After what seemed like hours but was probably just two minutes the bear decided we did not smell too tasty and he wandered off. Not three minutes later we heard our neighbors at the next site yelling, "GET OUT OF HERE!" They chose to yell at the bear after we remained silent.

We were too high on adrenalin or cortisol to sleep but had some whisky in the tent which soothed us. Bill confided he was about to slash the screen window on his end of the tent to make a mad dash for safety and Doug reported that he was so close to the bear's head he could see the hair in the animal's nostrils! After quite a bit of whiskey Doug and I finally got to sleep but I think Bill was awake all night. Bill thought the bear would be back, but I maintained it wouldn't since it consumed the only thing edible in our area - greasy dirt. The critter did not return that night, luckily.

The next morning when we were cooking breakfast on our Coleman stove the park ranger arrived to clean our privy. When we told him what happened the night before he remarked, "your campsite has the most bear contact of any in the park!" Holy crap! By the way, he also told us he has seen a bear climb a tree to rip down a rope holding a campers food bag! We could tell he was serious.

After a brief confab we decided to depart early. We packed up camp, trailered the boat and drove to Ely, Minnesota where we checked into a nice, safe motel. For two days we fished Lake

Shagawa on the edge of town. Bill had fished this lake previously with some other guys and had good luck in the spring.

However, it was 90 degrees and fishing was terrible. At one point, I got so over heated I jumped out of the boat with my clothes on just to cool off. My wetness kept me cool for a good while. We came home with few fish but some good stories, as usual. We never returned to that park. Not too hard to figure out why.

In the summer of 1994, a young fishing buddy and I joined the Midwest Fishing League out of St. Cloud. Tony was an avid angler and we got along well so we paired up. Our club had about 12 boats and we all fished together on area lakes each Wednesday night. One evening I caught a 13-pound pike on a green spoon. When we got to the access at the end of the night, I held up my catch to the guys with my white cane in the other hand. They asked if I caught it and I replied, "Yes, so it's a braille northern!" We laughed and I ended up with a little trophy that fall for catching the biggest fish in the League. We should have gotten another trophy for boating that fish since we forgot our net.

A couple of days later the League's founder, Duane, called me and asked if I would submit to a photo op and interview from a reporter from the St. Cloud Times. I agreed and the next Wednesday the photojournalist was waiting for me on the dock. We launched my boat and as Tony was holding it to the dock the guy took a photo of me tying on a jib. He asked me not to pose, just do something natural that I would normally do. He then asked me questions for about 15 minutes which he recorded. He asked my permission to put it all in the Times and I consented with the caveat that I wanted him to include my philosophy of blindness. He agreed and recorded the following one liner: "Blindness is an inconvenience that is occasionally frustrating and sometimes hilarious."

The article and photo appeared in the paper a few days later. My secretary found it and pinned it up in the coffee room. Fifteen minutes of fame?

My 4-year-old nephew's first fishing was in 1996 ice fishing on Independence Lake in the south area of the Twin Cities. Although we caught very few fish Tyler loved being out there with his dad and uncle Dan. He was curious about everything especially the power augers operating all around us.

In March of 1995, we decided to go to the Rainy River on the Canadian border to catch sturgeon. Roger and another guy wanted to get there at dawn from St. Cloud, Minnesota. I got up at 2:30 a.m. and slept in the back of their SUV all the way to the border while they were driving in the snowfall which they did not mind. We stopped at Lucky's Bait to buy 1-ounce jigs since the current was so strong that time of year. We fished all day and caught nothing but had a big one on. The highlight was pulling my boat up onto the ice on the edge of the river which was very strange. We took photos and I was a little nervous the boat point might break thru the shore ice, but it held. This is the only time my boat rested on ice and I never went back to the Rainy River.

In the summer of 1995, we decided to try something new. We ventured to Lake Sakakawea in western North Dakota but we did it in a weird way.

One morning roger and I took off in his Explorer while pulling his little trailer but without my boat. The plan was for Doug and Ross To meet us with my van and boat the next morning at a café in Garrison, ND where Roger's brother Bill lived at the time.

Just a few miles east of Garrison our little trailer that was carrying a 15 hp motor and heavy gear ended up on the side of our vehicle at 75 mph! We were jerking around all over the road before he managed to pull the rig onto the shoulder! It was a miracle we did not roll. When we inspected the trailer, we could see the axle was broken into. Bill was out of town so could not rescue us. After lots of nervous brainstorming we decided to leave me behind on I 94 to guard our belongings and the trailer while Roger drove into town for help. I really did not want to be left behind, but I did not want my outboard to be stolen off the shoulder and there was not room for it in his vehicle.

Roger promised me he would be back asap so I grudgingly agreed. So, there I was sitting in my lawn chair on the shoulder of a cross country interstate highway with a motor, a big cooler and my gear bag and the trailer. It was mostly semis flying by at 85 mph. The air draft they brought with them nearly knocked me over every time, not to mention the cloud of dust along for the ride. I thought to myself I must look totally silly sitting there in the middle of the hot, desolate prairie with a few items. A few people honked but no one stopped. After an hour or so I was getting nervous I might be there for many hours. It was also a hot, sunny day but at least I had beverages.

Roger finally came back. I was so happy to see him I gave him a hug. Somehow, he convinced a guy in Garrison to come with his flatbed truck to retrieve the trailer. Sure enough, a little while later the truck arrived. The three of us loaded the trailer onto the flatbed along with the motor. It turned out that guy was a mechanic who fixed the trailer that week when we were fishing. He only charged $110. Unbelievable.

The next morning at dawn we met Doug and ross at the café to dine and lay out our plan of attack. They were amazed at our story. By the way, they drove all night with my van and boat in spectacular lightning storms which they could see for 50 miles on the prairie! We then drove to Indian Hills Resort to pitch our tents. We did not get on the water until afternoon and hardly caught anything. We did not know how to fish reservoirs.

The next morning at breakfast the resort owner came to tell us that Bill was in the hospital so Roger took off to Garrison to check on his brother. We fished all day without him. The water was very murky in some areas and less so in others. Doug said he did not want to fish the dirty water as he thought walleyes would not be there. We only caught a few fish but had a nice fish fry that night. After supper we went to the resort office where there was a message from Roger to call him. I called him and learned that Bill's appendix had burst and he was in bad shape after surgery! Roger needed to be with Bill so he would not join us for a couple of days. Such luck!

The highlight of this trip was the dock girl who was the daughter of the owners. She was a gorgeous, buxom blond who looked a lot like Suzanne Summers! Doug always got up before us so he would drive my boat the short distance to the resort main dock for ice, gas and bait. Every morning that young woman jiggled her way to the dock to serve him although not quite in the way he wanted. She always wore a pink tank top with no bra, short shorts that showed her cute butt and little red sandals. She also had a sexy smile and was very friendly. She obviously knew what fishermen wanted. One morning Doug drove the boat there three time; each time claiming he forgot something. I am sure she was on to him, and she certainly enjoyed showing herself off to him especially when she bent forward to hand him something. Her big boobs nearly fell out and she would shake them in front of him. He smiled a lot in the morning.

Fishing was lousy all week. We found out from the guys at the next campsite on our last day that they got their walleyes in the murky water! They said the stained water provided nice cover for the fish so they congregated in it. We gave Doug a hard time about this since he refused to drive my boat into those waters. Sure enough, as soon as we fished the dirty water that day we filled out. I hope we learned our lesson.

Furthermore, we were supposed to pick up Roger at our campsite dock at noon but Doug did not tell us this so we did not come in until supper time. By then Roger had been waiting all afternoon. We left a bottle of brandy on the picnic table and Roger had drank a lot of it and was drunk. He claimed he did not drink it and it must have been a wayward passerby who guzzled the swill. We knew better but did not mind since he was always more fun when drunk. Bill survived but we never went back to Sakakawea. Too far for eater walleyes but we were glad we tried this new adventure. We made it home without further incidents, trailer in tow.

In the 1990's Doug and I were back on Lake Mille Lacs again, this time for some night fishing. We were on 7 Mile flats using lighted slip bobbers. Doug was naughty, using two lines which is illegal in Minnesota except on the ice. There was a massive school of baitfish under the boat and one of his rods was an ultralight lying on the bottom of the boat with the line in the water. When he picked it up to check his bait, he felt a heavy weight, so he set the hook. It was a good long fight with the fish staying straight down so we knew it was a large walleye. When he finally netted it, we could see with our lantern and boat light it was a wall hanger! It weighed in at 9 pounds on the nose. We yelled and high fived! We were especially surprised that we caught this lunker in late August which was "dog days" and usually slow for walleyes. That fish still hangs on Doug's wall to this day.

On October 1, 1995 roger and I drove from St. Cloud to Bemidji for two days. Someone gave us a hot fishing tip about a hidden lake called Rabideau, which is just off the Pennington Road to Blackduck, Minnesota. Early that morning we drove nearly all the way around this small two-part lake on a gravel road. The trees formed a tunnel over the road and their leaves were orange. Roger and I marveled at the beauty of driving through an orange tunnel. It was surreal. When we finally found the boat access down a steep hill, we saw a black bear cub on the water's edge. Upon further observation we noticed he was eating a dead fish. We have enough wildlife lore to know the mother sow was probably nearby so we waited in the vehicle until he left. Then as we backed the trailer down the hill, we honked the horn all the way with hopes that would scare the bruins far away. When we got the boat over the water roger took a good look around and saw no bears. We unloaded the boat, parked the vehicle, and took off quickly with a shove off since there was no dock. It did not take too long to find a school of the biggest sunfish we ever saw. We fished right under the boat without bobbers; just hooks with rainbow minnows. We caught many sunnies over a pound. After n hour or two we started throwing back sunfish that only weighed 1.25 pounds as they were too small! The live well was getting loaded with big ones and we boated some crappies that pushed two pounds in 20-28 feet of water. It started snowing and the fishing really got nuts. It was instant bites every time we dropped a bait in that depth range. We could not believe our good fortune! We had a scale and several of the sunfish weighed two pounds on the nose! They were bigger than the few crappies we boated. We never caught sunfish on rainbows before as they are usually too big for the tiny mouths of the sunfish.

The sunfish limit back then was thirty and we probably had 50 big panfish in the live well when we decided to quit fishing. It was late afternoon and we were tired and frozen from fishing in the snow all day. By then we had two inches of snow in the boat. When we got back to the Best Western, we put the fish in my cooler with lots of ice and dragged it into our room.

By ten o'clock Roger fell asleep. I patiently stayed awake to call Doug right after midnight when he got off work. I told him he should drive up tonight since he will never get another chance to catch 2-pound sunfish. Even the pumpkinseeds weighed 1.5

pounds, I told him. He didn't believe me about the size of the fish but agreed to join us. He woke up his wife, my sister, to tell her he was leaving for 24 hours since he did not have to work the next day. He took some No-Doze and left Anoka.

He drove all night and got to the hotel at dawn. Roger just happened to be in the lobby getting coffee when Doug walked in. Roger could not believe his eyes and said, "Doug, what the hell are you doing here?' Doug told him about the phone call from me and they came to our room together with coffee. When Doug looked into the cooler he gasped. He said he has never seen sunfish that size before. Neither had we!

On the way out of town we went through a drive-up window for breakfast. This time when we got to the Lake Webster road, it was very foggy driving through the orange tunnel. This made it both eerie and breathtakingly beautiful. Super surreal!

When we finally got on the water, without any bears in the area, we found the fish near to that same spot. We immediately started pounding the same size fish which were a blast on our ultralight rods. We fished into the afternoon and decided we probably had close to three limits between those in the live well and those in the cooler in the vehicle. We all drove to my house in St. Cloud to clean our catch. We had to call our friend Ken V. to help us clean them all which took three hours. We took some great photos including some of the live well packed to the top with fish. We all knew this was an experience of a lifetime and that we would never find pan-fishing like this again. It turned out we were right as we went back to Lake Rabideau several times since, but the bonanza was over. We caught few fish and they were nothing like the ones of 1995. After that two days of glory fishing, we heard rumors of a freeze out on Rabideau. We just happened to be in the right place at the right time, finally!

In the spring of 1996 when Ty was four and a half, we had him in my boat for the first time. He was so short he could barely see over the gunnels of my Smokercraft boat. We were bobber fishing for panfish. Tyler's bobber went down so Doug showed him how to set the hook. When Doug gave the rod back to him, he could barely crank the handle of his Snoopy reel. We knew from the bend of the rod it was no bluegill or crappie. It took a long time but we let the boy play it out. Doug netted the four-pound largemouth bass. Tyler stated, "I love to catch fish!" Doug and I smiled at each other, realizing at the same time that all our efforts to get Tyler hooked on fishing had finally paid off. We high fived in the boat! It was a glorious day!

In June of 1997, Doug, Tyler, and I were fishing Lake Mille Lacs out of Agate Bay Resort. At that time there was a 10 pm curfew on the water. At 9:45 many boats headed for the dock at the same time, including us. We were idling in line right after dusk and were very close to the dock. A vehicle was trying to back their trailer into the water to pull out their boat. It was two old guys, and the driver was struggling to back it correctly in the dark onto a very narrow ramp. It took several attempts and the onlookers were getting very impatient and started yelling at the old guy behind the wheel which was upsetting for us to watch. Suddenly, the entire trailer and half the vehicle went into the water! The driver slumped over his steering wheel and did not move again. The guy in the passenger's seat started yelling for help. The people who were yelling at the driver were now the ones dragging him out of his car and onto the dock where he was unresponsive.

My boat and the boat next to mine were touching so we were holding onto each other as the horrifying spectacle unfolded before us. Doug jumped out of the boat and onto the dock. He started doing CPR on the old guy for a long time with another first responder. Tyler was only five and did not know what was going on so I just told him his dad was helping a sick man. The ambulance finally arrived nearly 30 minutes later and by then Doug had revived the poor man and he was breathing again. However, the old angler died in the ambulance. The EMT's called the resort to say he perished and he told us the sad news just as we were finally pulling away. Just before we left for home his friend said his fishing buddy would have wanted to die on a fishing trip anyway which was small consolation since we all felt terrible.

It was a sad ride home. Doug was shook up and needed to talk but I was fighting to stay awake since it was now well after midnight. Tyler slept all the way home to St. Cloud. We both agreed that the jerks who yelled at the old guy should feel bad that they stressed him out at the wheel, but he might have died anyway. We were disappointed and surprised that some anglers would be so mean. We wondered why they did not volunteer to help him back his trailer instead of yelling at him. I guess there is a dark side of fishing too. The special camaraderie between anglers that I mentioned earlier does not apply to all of them, unfortunately.

Except for this tragic event, 1997 was a great fishing year for me. I went fishing thirty times that year and some of those trips were multiple days on the water. I fished over two dozen lakes I was never on before. This is the most fishing days I ever had, before or since.

As my eyesight continued to worsen, I was forced to adapt so I could maintain my angling therapy. When I was 15, with normal vision, a Filipino pastor taught me how to tie a fisherman's knot. I did this thousands of times so I got to the point where I could do it well although I could no longer see the monofilament or lure or swivel snap. I learned to do it just by using my fingers and tongue. I needed little help in the boat; just rare bird nests in my reel but mostly just help with identifying colors. The most difficult thing was threading the line through a slip bobber at which I could rarely succeed.

Starting in the 1990's I began tying up my own spinners of all colors which was very time consuming but always worked. I greatly enjoy doing things that blind people are not supposed to be able to do. In fact, Ralph Waldo Emerson once stated that one of life's greatest joys is doing things that others say we cannot do. You are correct, Mr. E!

It came in handy that I could tie knots without eyesight since we sometimes fished in the dark and the guys in my boat struggled with knots in low light from the boat's dim light pole. I usually rubbed it in that I might have to tie knots for them. Furthermore, I suspect I am one of the few blind boat owners in Minnesota, if not the only one, and am a little bit proud of this.

In June of 1998 we went back to the English River which by now we nicknamed the English riviera. There were five of us in two boats and we camped on cemetery island again. It was always a wild and wacky adventure on that big water. One beautiful day we made the mistake of bringing a bottle of tequila in my boat for which I might take some of the blame. After a couple shots with lemon slices, we were not feeling any pain, but we decided it would be easier to drop the anchor and slip bobber fish instead of trolling. I remember boating a six-pound walleye that afternoon and things got a little blurry after that.

Those of us in my boat did not protect ourselves from the sun that day like we usually do. We got very sunburned. The next day I took a lot of ibuprofen for the pain and I had to drape a rag over both hands and one over my head to keep the hot sun off my blistered lips and backs of my hands. Doug said I looked like a ghost. I felt pretty stupid and humbled by my painful mistake.

We always had a jackpot for the biggest walleye and the biggest pike. On the last night we had an award ceremony on the island. Doug had the biggest walleye and Dave the biggest pike. They stood on the point and walked up to the rest of us who were waiting with a bottle of champagne. We serenaded them with our two wooden flutes and saluted them and even bowed to them. It was hilarious and we topped off the evening by lighting a giant cigar. We passed it around for 45 minutes even though it was very stale and had a nasty bite. It was a grand evening and Terry even read a little poem he composed that week for the occasion. The champagne was great too.

In July of 1998, I went to Lake of the Woods with a cabbie named Charlie. We went in his RV and pulled his big boat. He did not know the way to Baudette, Minnesota and did not have a map. We got lost twice. As soon as we got on the water he got lost again. We drove around for an hour on Zippel Bay trying to get oriented. Unfortunately, he had no compass either. He made the classic mistake of not eyeballing our resort as we pulled away from the access. On top of that he grabbed the wrong carton out of his fridge and we ended up with peanut butter in the boat instead of nightcrawlers! To complicate matters, his new locator did not work. He speculated that he forgot to pull the plastic strip off the new transducer. Since we could not reach it from inside the boat, I volunteered to get in the water to check it out. Charlie did not know how to swim. I stripped off my clothes and jumped into the lake, glad it was July instead of May or October. Alas, the transducer was free of plastic and seemed to be positioned correctly. Somehow, I crawled back into his boat.

We only caught two walleyes that day. The next day Charlie drove between two buoys at high speed and we crashed. He broke off his skag and bent up the big prop. The impact also cracked the housing of his outboard's lower unit. To top things off, I broke my favorite Fenwick spinning rod. When we were pulling out the boat Charlie backed his trailer off the side of the concrete ramp. We had a devil of a time getting the trailer back onto the ramp but finally succeeded.

I was happy when this weekend trip was over and felt relieved. I decided Chevy Chase could have made one of his comical movies out of this fishing disaster: "Lake of the Woods Fishing

Vacation"; coming soon to a theatre near you. It turned out that Charlie and I never went fishing together again and I was okay with that. Whew!

In the 1990's, Doug and his son Tyler and I fished Sauk Lake many times. It was a very good lake just outside of Sauk Centre, Minnesota. We caught lots of good crappies as well as walleyes and bluegills. We usually fished until just before dusk and then drove home to St. Cloud in the dark after stopping at McDonalds for supper. Tyler was only 5 or 6 years old at the time and was still afraid of the dark so he would not sit in the back of my van by himself. He always ended up sitting on my lap and usually fell asleep. When we got to my house Doug would carry him up to his bed and then we would clean our catch. We did this sweet adventure many times and still have fond, heart-warming memories of them.

Early in 1997, Doug and I went ice fishing on Lake of the Woods out of Randall's Resort. It was another wild angling adventure! We had two sets of bunk beds on one end of the fish house and one morning when I was sleeping in Doug had an exhilarating experience. He hooked something huge that took control of his rod and reel. He worked it for a long time and finally managed to hoist the brute up to the hole. When he looked down the hole, he saw that the head of the giant sturgeon was much too large for the 8-inch hole! When he looked down the hole that was six feet away, he saw the tail. While running back and forth he knocked over the kitchen table which woke me up.

Shortly afterwards, the leviathan threw the jib jook and escaped, damn it. When Doug showed me the jib, its hook was straight as a pin! I have never seen that before.

In May of 1997, Doug, Ross and I decided to open the walleye season on Lake Mille lacs again. We hit the water at 11 pm that Friday night to wait for the season to open at midnight. We put in at Agate Bay Resort, one of our favorites. There were already lots of boats on the water. We fished for hours and caught 13 walleyes. About 3 in the morning, I took a nap in the front of my boat. When I woke at day break there were snow flurries on the lake. Nevertheless, we fished until 9 pm that night which gave us 22 hours on the water. We only came off the water once in the afternoon to clean our catch and use the resort bathroom. It was a great marathon but we were younger then and could never do that now.

In August of 1997, Roger and I were fishing Pike Bay near Cass Lake, Minnesota. The water was perfectly still with some drizzle. We were just sitting there with the anchor in the boat. No boat movement at all which is unusual. Roger, who is not usually a heavy drinker, decided to get drunk in the boat, perhaps due to boredom and rain. The fishing was dead and he eventually passed out on the floor of my boat. Shortly thereafter, I hooked a nice fish on the bottom in 53 feet of water using a slip sinker and snell hook with a leech. It was a good fight and took me a while to get it to the surface. I knew I would not be able to net it myself so I woke roger which wasn't easy. He netted the 5-pound walleye and went right back to sleep. It was a beautiful bay with lots of wildlife. I enjoyed the tranquility.

In the summer of 1998 Ross, Doug and I went to the English River for the second time that summer. The allure of the place was magical so we just could not stay away. We drove all night to get there. We arrived at Gosh Hawk landing at daybreak. The local Chippewa folks were nowhere to be found. We dared not leave our van and trailer without paying them so we waited two hours before they showed up at their cabin by the access. In the meantime, we loaded everything into my Smokercraft so we could make a quick getaway once we paid up. While waiting we were serenaded by very loud, traditional Native chanting and drumming music. It was very beautiful, and the sound filled the forest. It turned out they had a greenhouse a couple of blocks away and they were apparently serenading their plants. Since I have always had an affinity for Native culture I really enjoyed sitting on the dock and listening despite the voracious and large mosquitos. It was both eerie and spiritual for me. We have never experienced this phenomenon here before or since.

At about 8 a.m. Rosie, a middle-aged Native woman, finally showed up. We paid her and, as usual, she hugged and kissed us all. She also showed a photo of a beautiful Indian girl who was her daughter. She told us the daughter suicided a few months earlier. She got tearful and we gave her more hugs. We felt sorry for her and this confirmed that Native Americans and Native Canadians have a very high suicide rate especially among young people. The girl was only 18

As usual, we caught tons of walleyes. One afternoon we found a bay full of sumps sticking out of the water. We motored into an open area and spent the entire afternoon backtrolling in a tight circle and catching dozens of walleyes. The beer was great too. After throwing fish on the stringer for hours, we lost count.

When we got back to our island, we discovered we had 22 walleyes on the stringer: four more than the legal limit for three guys. We cleaned them all and had a huge fish meal that night which put us down to 18 fish so we were legal. We still have fond memories of Stump Bay as we named it! We got them all on spinners, up to five pounds.

It was the summer of 1998, when Doug, Tyler and I went to camp at Clint converse Campground on Lake Washburn just north of Crosby, MN. When we got to the camp it was raining. We sat in the van for an hour waiting for it to let up so we could pitch our tent and cots. Tyler was only 6 at the time and very restless sitting in the van. Finally, I put on my rain suit and then put an adult rain jacket on the boy which came down to his feet. I rolled up the sleeves and tied on his hood. We then put his boots on and got out to play in the rain. I did three cartwheels in the rain even though I could not see the ground. This delighted little Tyler. He had never seen a cartwheel before and screamed with delight. He attempted several cartwheels but flopped on his back every time, which made him giggle even more. The rain finally let up and we erected the tent. We guessed that not too many blind people have ever turned cartwheels in the rain. Yes, I was sober.

Fishing was lousy that weekend but I taught Ty how to skip rocks and he loved it. When he got the hang of it, he did not want to stop and ended up skipping rocks for a whole hour while his dad was cleaning our meager catch.

The adjacent campsite was held by a family with a little black dog named Figero. He played with that pup all week and I think they fell in love with each other. It was so cute.

In June of 1999, five of us went back to the English riviera. It included Doug, Ross, myself and a high school friend Dave as well as Doug's friend, Mark. We had two boat this time and managed to pay the Natives to camp on their cemetery island and fish their waters once again. Rosie was the Chippewa lady who ran the private access business. She loved to hug and kiss us and said, "at least you white boys have hairy chests!"

We made it out to the island with no trouble on the huge One Man Lake. However, when I was sitting next to a gas can on the 12-mile drive to our island I got soaked with gasoline. Someone left the vent hole unplugged when filling up a can and when we hit a wave some gas shot out and got my pants wet right by my butt. In just a couple of minutes the gas was burning my skin so I took off my pants as we were cruising at full throttle. I wiped off the gas with a wet rag but noticed my underwear were wet with gas too! I took them off and threw them up into the air and into the lake right in front of our other boat. Of course, since I was naked from the waist down, I could not resist the temptation to moon my fellow anglers. Mark said later that when he saw my underwear fly into the air, he knew it would be a wild trip. Indeed, it was since we usually regress to adolescence on our trips!

Mark bought with him a tiny suitcase that carried his wife's falsies! She had just had breast enlargement surgery and did not need the fake ones any longer. One day he nailed those rubber boobs onto a birch tree near our tent. They stayed there for years and we were always proud of him for his heroism!

On that same trip Mark was casting for pike when he hooked a huge one. The brute swam all the way around the boat twice at high speed. Mark and Doug were lunging around the boat trying to keep up and to net it. When Doug finally netted it, we weighed it at 22 pounds! We released it unharmed after some admiring photos. Amazingly, he caught it on a medium action spinning rod with only 10-pound test monofilament. At least he was using a leader which probably saved the catch.

We have always had the tradition of allowing the angler who caught a big one to name that spot if it did not already have a name. Mark named that spot Mark's Hole. Yikes! See what I mean about regressing?

We wore out that spot and found a little river we never noticed previously. As we motored into it slowly, we spotted two moose on the water's edge. It was a cow and a baby moose, and they were sticking their heads into the water to eat moss and slime off the submerged rocks. They fled as soon as they saw us, of course. As we entered a small bay that we never saw before we got excited since we figured it must be loaded with large, hungry fish. While one boat was trolling crankbaits above the weeds we were casting out of mine. Dave was using a rattlin' rap and boated a six-pound walleye. I was using a Panther Martin 280 sonar lure which the fish would not leave alone. I caught several large walleyes, pike and smallmouth bass on that rare lure that day. Unfortunately, I lost it and was never able to buy any more anywhere.

It was on this trip that we decided to ring in the new millennium of 2000 with a fly in fishing adventure. We spent one evening around the campfire planning it out which in itself was exciting.

In July of 1999 Doug, Tyler and I were angling lake Mille Lacs again, which was our favorite since we usually did so well there. However, this time it was a Murphy's Law day. After fishing in the drizzle most of the day, somehow both marine batteries died out. We had no lights, no tilt & trim, no locator and were adrift. Since we could not crank up the 60 horse Mariner we eventually lodged on some rocks in the south of Garrison Bay. We had to wave down a nearby boat and they towed us in at about 10 pm to Garrison public access. We drove a few miles with the Mariner down to Moline's Trophy sports bar and got two drunk guys to lend us their battery which we used to crank up the motor. It was a humbling experience and we were just happy to be alive and well. Some of our fishing excursions had lots of adversity as you can see.

In the late 1990's, Roger and I went to a lake in the St. Cloud area. It was a slow day on the water but we stuck it out until late afternoon anyway. As my boat neared the dock roger said there was a lady game warden waiting to make sure all boat owners were checking their rigs for milfoil. We got the boat on the trailer and pulled over to put all our gear in my van. As I was standing next to my boat, white cane in hand, roger warned, "here she comes. Pretend you are searching for milfoil!" I handed my white cane to him and crawled under my rig. I felt the bottom of the boat and trailer and even pretended like I found some weeds. Then we jumped in my van and pulled away. At that point we both realized Roger forgot to give me my cane and I forgot to ask for it. He jumped into the driver's seat with it in hand!

As we drove away, Roger looked in the rear-view mirror. The lady game warden was staring at us with mouth agape! No doubt she thought a blind man was driving my rig! We laughed all the way home. What made it even more comical is the fact that we did not plan this; it just happened that way.

The next day Roger went back to that same public access with another friend since I had to work. That lady was still there so he went up to talk with her so he could explain the faux paux. She made a point of watching the 10 o'clock news the night before, certain she would hear a tragic story about a god-awful car accident involving a blind driver! They laughed for quite a while. This is yet another example of the crazy things that can happen with a blind angler.

CHAPTER FOUR: DEER SHACKING THE 1990'S

In June of 1991 Doug, Ross and I went to the deer shack owned by Doug's relative. That Saturday night the Minnesota North Stars were in the Stanley Cup finals. After catching a lot of nice crappies in Lake Emily in Emily, Minnesota, we stopped at the Broken Arrow Bar & Grill in Outing for beer, food and hockey on the big screen. We got the last three open bar stools as the place was packed and there was high excitement about the game since hockey is a big deal in Minnesota.

The beer went down well but the only food was appetizers that were deep fried. We ordered the giant combination platter and wolfed it down. After the game which the Stars won, we went back to the shack. We were still hungry so Doug fried up some burgers while Ross was outside throwing up for quite a while. He always had a weak stomach and all the fried food was too much for it. To make matters worse, he picked nine wood tics off himself while barfing.

Doug has a brother-in-law named Walter who owned that nice deer shack about 20 miles north of Crosby, Minnesota. It's just 50 feet from a bullhead hole named Lake George which was full of loons. The loon is the Minnesota state bird and has beautiful bird song as you probably know. We loved listening to the loon call all night on the water. This structure rests on many heavily wooded acres and has a large picture window.

For Labor Day weekend in 1997, Doug and I took Tyler there for the first time. He was only five and a half and had no idea what a deer shack was. He got very excited that it had bunks, a table and chairs, and even an old Norge fridge that made a lot of weird noises, as well as a LP cook stove. The bunks even had thick pad so we thought it was the Ritz. The shack had electricity but no running water, so we always carted in our own. It also had an outhouse with an outside light. Tyler was terrified of the outhouse and never used it all weekend. He just wouldn't go near it.

We always brought a table radio in the deer shack so we could listen to the Power Loon station out of Brainerd. The first thing we heard that next morning was that Princess Diana died in a car crash in Paris. Doug said, "Oh boy, major news hits the deer shack! I suppose Di won't come to the deer shack after all now." He always had a silly fantasy that the Princess might join us there some day but maintained that she did not show up just because the outhouse was not new enough for royalty. He maintained if it was new and fancy with bells and whistles, she might just put in a cameo appearance someday. Alas, the poor doll never made it. We reasoned that if she had visited us that fateful weekend, she would still be alive. LOL

On our first day of fishing, we were on Lake Washburn, which is a party lake, just a few miles away. We caught lots of bluegills and Tyler was in all his glory. Unfortunately, he had to poop. We did not want to drive him to shore so he pooped his little turd in an empty donut box right in the boat. He thought this was great fun and laughed about it all weekend. In fact, when he got home, he talked about that more than the fishing!

We started out on Lake George the next morning even though it was a bullhead hole but we were hoping there would be some nice bluegills mixed with the horned slimers but to no avail. We boated bullhead after bullhead and eventually filled a 5-gallon pail with them. My hands were numb from being stung by them but it wore off after a while. We only caught one sunfish. After an hour we left the little lake and dumped the dead bullheads at the dockless access. We wanted to clean some out of that lake and we figured the local critters would happily chomp down on the dead fish like they always do.

The next day we drove up to Sugar Lake by Remer which is less developed than Washburn. We kept 50 sunfish and had great weather. I even went skinny-dipping by jumping out of the boat since it was a hot day with no boats around.

We have many fond memories in that shack such as waking to the smell of brewing coffee and frying bacon. In fact, one morning when Doug was doing that very thing, a mouse ran right over the top of his foot. He tried to stomp it but it was too fast. Lucky for him, he had his shoes on. Somehow, we usually lucked out and had little rain. There are more stories to come about the hallowed deer shack which was also a fine home for mice. We always brought D-Con to feed the hungry critters. It was the least we could do.

On another trip to the venerable deer shack it was my brother Jeff, Doug, Ross, and myself. One evening after supper we were playing quarter ante poker. Jeff had a coin box on the table. It should be noted that he is terrified of frogs. Sure enough, when Ross went outside to urinate instead of throwing up, he spotted a frog. He brought it into the shack with a finger over his lips to shush us. He put the frog in Jeff's coin box and sat down to play. It wasn't long before Jeff had to make a bet and toss some coins into the kitty bowl. When he touched the frog is squirmed and jumped! Jeff jumped up, nearly knocking over the table, and yelled in terror! He cussed us out at the top of his lungs and ran outside to get away and cool off. When the mosquitos got bad, he came back in and we threw out the frog. He was pouting a little but was able to laugh about it later that night after some brandy.

Ross is terrified of bats so you know what happened. Later that same night when he was outside trying to decide if he should pee or vomit a bat dive-bombed his head. He yelled and stormed into the shack like a raging bull. We couldn't decide if it was poetic justice or some kind of weird karma, but Jeff certainly got a kick out of it and did a lot of snickering. This we call male bonding! A grand time was had by all that night too.

On another deer shack adventure in the 1990's we had the same crew of ne'er do wells. We did not take Tyler on all these trips until later in this decade since he was a toddler. We fished Lake Trellipe just a few miles north of the shack. It was a remote lake that was undeveloped except for a farm on one end. We usually caught big panfish but never lots of them. Occasionally, we would catch a fish with a growth which we attributed to agricultural runoff from that farm. We never kept those but were happy to eat other fish from that lake. It was a nice change from the busy party Lake Washburn. The girl watching was best on Washburn, however. We always had the best luck for panfish with Mini-Mite jigs.

One night we had a nice campfire while drinking beer until the wee hours. Doug was sitting on the fish cleaning table when we heard a loud crack and he went down. He did not get hurt except for a sliver in his fat butt. We assured him we definitely would not help remove that sliver. The table burned quite nicely though. He told the owner later that some teenagers must have burned it up.

That same night, for some reason, Doug climbed to the top of the shack to watch the debauchery from a bird's eye vantage point. All the while we were listening to Pink Floyd's "Dark Side of the Moon" at high volume on my boom box. There was never anyone in the woods with us so we could get as rowdy as we wished. While perched on the roof, Doug observed Jeff barfing which ignited a disgusting chain reaction which caused Ross to upchuck too. We decided to put the barfers to bed, tucked them in and kissed them good night. Yuck!

We made many trips to the legendary deer shack throughout the 90's and into the next decade. Tyler fell in love with it right away. Unfortunately, Walter sold it in the 2000's. We were sad about this and still miss it to this day. However, we have many fond memories of those great times there and it was a step up from sleeping in a tent. The roof didn't even leak!

CHAPTER FIVE: MILLE LACS RATS

I have shared a few fishing adventures above about Lake Mille Lacs but since there are so many, I decided to devote a chapter just to this great body of water. I have probably fished this lake a hundred times, not always with good luck. Unfortunately, the lake got fished out due to over harvesting and invasive species so now I have not fished it in ten years. It is a sad outcome and I miss it to this day.

Many resorts, cafes and other businesses on the lake have closed up due to very few anglers and campers. For decades it was a thriving economy which supported many jobs. There are two state parks on the lake as well as a casino and Chippewa museum which are still open and run by the local Mille Lacs band of Chippewa, right off their reservation.

At the end of the 90's decade Doug, Ross and I again opened the walleye season on Lake Mille lacs. We hit the water just before the season opened at midnight that Friday. We fished all night again just like so many anglers. The guys could see hundreds of tiny boat lights on poles scattered all around the lake which is 132,500 acres. We were in the area off the little fishing mecca of Garrison, Minnesota. In the middle of the night, we heard a loudspeaker deep male voice which startled us. At first, I thought God was talking to us but no such luck. It was only an earthly game warden who snuck up on us with a super quiet inboard motor. He said they were watching us with a night scope and noticed Doug was fishing with two lines which is unlawful in the land of sky-blue waters.

Doug replied, "that one is just dangling, officer." The narc retorted, "it's doing more than dangling, sir, so you are getting a citation." Doug got a ticket for $70, which he had to pay to Crow Wing County. He was pretty quiet the rest of the night but he learned his lesson and never used two lines again.

In the late 90's in the month of June we went nuts on Mille Lacs fishing. We drove from St. Cloud to that lake two nights in a row and caught plenty of fish and kept a few. It was night fishing on Agate Bay reef. We usually fished with lighted slip bobbers until 2 or 3 a.m. We got home at dawn and took the next night off. Then we went back for another night of catching walleyes on the rocks. We fished 3 out of 4 nights. It was Roger, Mike and I and Doug came up from the Cities for the last night. We did not get into any trouble those nights and no one died.

In the late 1990's during the month of October Roger and I drove to Mille Lacs hoping to hit the frog run which causes walleyes to put on the old feed bag. He and I lived in St. Cloud, Minnesota at that time and it was only a 60-minute drive to the east side of the lake. It was very cold that fall night so we were bundled up in our ice fishing clothing. We motored to Doe Island and dropped anchor in a small bay where he saw the frog run once before. We were only in four feet of water when we began casting with the anchor down. It wasn't long before we saw a few big walleyes jumping out of the water! Roger took my lantern and shone it on the surface. He said the damn fish were jumping up and shaking their heads back and forth. After studying them for a while he said the walleyes had fish tales hanging out of their maws and did the head shake apparently to get the meal down their gullet! He said they looked like tullibee that were being ravaged by the walleyes. It turned out that the tullibee were spawning in that bay and the predator fish were going nuts feeding on them. We had never seen walleyes so aggressive! They acted like they were starving. We saw and heard hundreds of them jumping up and shaking their heads.

We threw everything we had at them. We casted crank baits that were similar color of the yellowish tullibees and also jigs and minnows. We even tried slip bobbers with minnows and casted spinners with nightcrawlers. All to no avail. At one point he shone the light into the water right next to my boat and saw big fish just a couple of feet below the surface. He grabbed the landing net and tried several times to scoop them up but they were too fast and he never managed to land any. We watched this bizarre and unusual natural phenomenon for two hours before we gave up and departed. We talked to other anglers about this, and they never heard of it either, including some dyed-in-the-wool Mille Lacs rats. We just happened to be in the right place at the right time. We did not mind at all that we got skunked since we knew we witnessed an amazing piscatorial event. We never encountered this scene again on that lake or any other.

In 2005, Ken, Dave and I went back to our favorite inland sea, Mille Lacs, for a hot afternoon of fishing. In July and August most of the walleyes, especially the bigger females, lived on the mud flats in the center of the lake. It was a sunny afternoon so we knew we would have to fish deep. We motored out to 9-mile flats which is a six-mile voyage. This structure is about a half mile wide and runs from 24 to 31 feet deep. There were plenty of boats on the flats but they were all trolling and catching nice eaters, smaller fish but big enough to keep for consumption. They were trolling the top of the flat in the shallowest water. We knew the bigger ones would be on the edge of the flats since they relate best to breaks, so we drove around for a while until we found a break at 29 feet deep. Right next to it was 31 feet. Sure enough, we spotted big fish on our locator. They were right off the bottom as usual. We lowered our power anchor to pinpoint the boat right on top of them which took some navigating since the boat would drift before the anchor finally got to the mud. At that point, we noticed no one else was anchored. I tied on a florescent white Gamakatsu hook and set my slip knot at twenty-seven feet or so. We knew that in the heat of summer walleyes love big baits so we bought jumbo leeches. I hooked one through the middle instead of the suction cup since this gives me a better chance of hooksets. Ken and Dave used the same strategy.

Sure enough, about ten minutes later Dave's bobber shot down. He paused briefly and set the hook by jerking straight up. His fish had lots of torque so we knew it was a nice one. After a sweet tussle of ten minutes duration Ken netted Dave's walleye. We measured it at 27 inches and seven pounds. We took a quick photo and released it unharmed. It swam away and we were happy it was only lip hooked. It was illegal to keep a fish that size in those waters. Just a few minutes later my bobber shot down too. Of course, I could not see it but I felt the tug. I pointed the rod tip down for about five seconds to give the fish time to swallow the leech. Then I reeled up the slack and slammed him. It was heavy but I played her out okay and got it to the surface. Dave netted the fish which weighed in at 7.5 pounds and 27.5 inches long. It was a bit bigger than Dave's and I released it too. We were happy it swam away instead of going belly up.

At this point, the boats around us moved in close, still trolling, apparently believing it was the spot we were on that produced the fish instead of the presentation. It was both. Just 15 minutes later Ken set the hook on another big fish right under the boat. He fought it for a while and Dave netted the beast. This weighed in at 8 pounds and 28 inches long, the biggest walleye Ken ever caught. Altogether we boated 22.5 pounds of walleyes in 45 minutes on just three fish. This happened between 3 pm and 3:45pm. People who believe walleyes cannot be caught on a sunny afternoon may be mistaken as this was not the only time we did this.

Despite witnessing our catch from an anchored boat, the other boats kept trolling. Walleyes are basically lazy, especially the big ones, and often want the bait standing still but the trollers did not seem to know this. We did not catch much the rest of the day but it was a glorious afternoon on the big pond.

CHAPTER SIX: MILLENNIUM FLY-IN FISHING ECSTASY

As noted above, when five of us went to the English River in 1999 we decided to ring in the new millennia of 2000 by embarking on a fly-in fishing trip to Ontario. None of us ever did this type of fishing adventure before and we were terribly excited about this prospect. We also decided we wanted to be on a lake where ours was the only cabin. We wanted lots of privacy and the whole lake to ourselves since we knew we would probably due this only once. Doug volunteered to take responsibility to find such a place.

That following winter he and I attended the All-Canada Fishing Show in Minneapolis to scout for such a resort. We talked to many outfitters and finally found one that sounded perfect for us. They had photos of nice cabins and the price was suitable so we took their literature and soon thereafter we paid our deposits to Northern Outposts. The sales rep said we would have two lakes to ourselves that were connected by a navigable stream. We jumped at this opportunity.

We signed up for the third week of June 2000. We drove north in two vehicles on a Friday and trailed each other to the Grand Portage, Minnesota border crossing. Doug was smuggling a gallon of brandy in a one gallon brand new gas can in the back of my van. I guess it never occurred to us that if we got searched at the border it might look suspicious that we had a gas can but no boat. Sure enough, we got searched and the agent confiscated Doug's brandy can since we were way over the meager limit. However, at least there was no fine and after making us wait a long time, which they always do, they waved us across.

At Thunder Bay, Ontario we turned north for the 3-hour drive to Armstrong which was literally the end of the road. Once we got north of Thunder Bay, we saw eight bears in the ditches eating blueberries. There was only one gas station along the way so we topped off. We checked into McKenzie motel in Armstrong and the clerk told us not to leave the motel after dark as the town fills up with foraging black bears. He said they come right up to the front door of the motel. We were amazed and realized we really were in the deep wilderness.

We checked in at Northern Outpost to pay up. We arranged to meet our bush pilot at the only restaurant in town for supper. He fit the stereotypical image of a grisly looking bush pilot but seems to know his stuff. He gave us directions to the air strip and said to be there at 5 a.m. the next day. The food was pretty good, but we were too excited to sleep much.

The next day we got up at 4 a.m. and took off without breakfast. We found the airstrip okay and began loading our gear onto the platform next to the plane. The pilot arrived just as we finished and then we carried everything onto the plane. It was still dark, and I wasn't able to help since I could not see anything, but the guys did not mind. As we took off the pilot told us the little puddle jumper was a 1958 Otter. We got a little nervous about that and hoped he would not say, "I don't know, boys. The engine just doesn't sound right today!" Yikes!

We achieved a cruising altitude of one mile and just then the sun peaked over the horizon. It was the first time any of us witnessed the sunrise from above and it was nothing short of spectacular. Even I could see it. We flew straight north for 70 minutes right over the Albany River. We flew over a little riverside village named Landdowner. The pilot said this village was only accessible by plane so most things had to be flown in. We marveled at how cut off they were from the civilized world and wondered what life was like there. We were grateful the flight was uneventful.

When we arrived at our designated lake, we thought it was too small to land on. However, the pilot got the little plane down okay at which time we all cheered. When he taxied up to the dock there were six crusty anglers waiting with all their belongings. We were also greeted by thick swarms of mosquitos hovering around the docks. Apparently, they were waiting for breakfast; namely us. The waiting anglers helped us unload our stuff, so we helped them carry their gear onto the plane while our pilot used the brand-new outhouse. The cabin had two bedrooms with two sets of bunk beds each. There was electricity from a solar powered generator. The bathroom had a sink and shower but no toilet. The finest outhouse we had ever seen was only about twenty feet from the cabin, however. We had a gas freezer, a gas refrigerator, and a gas stove. We had running water that came from the lake. It was filtered and tasted okay. We cooked some burgers and strong, black coffee for breakfast and got ready for fishing even though we were all exhausted and running on adrenalin.

Doug worked out a fishing schedule before the trip started so that each of us got to fish with a different guy each day. We had

14-foot boats with 10 horsepower gas motors. The boats were not equipped with locators or anchors. We were disappointed about the locators but soon discovered they were not necessary.

Our first day on the water I fished with Doug. We caught plenty of walleyes but no big ones. We were just learning our lake and did not get to the adjoining one. At one point in the afternoon, we stopped trolling and turned off the motor to drift fish and to give Doug a break from driving. I heard the sound of rushing water in the distance and mentioned it to Dug. It sounded like a waterfall so we went exploring. We found a little inlet that was ringed with lily pads with beautiful blossoms. There was a waterfall but only about three feet tall. This picturesque spot was the epitome of untouched Canadian wilderness that we loved so much.

Waterfalls wash feed into the water below which often draws in gamefish, so we dropped our lines into the water. There was no room to troll so we just sat there. Unfortunately, the walleyes did not know they are supposed to be schooled up in that spot, so we caught none. Nevertheless, I was reluctant to depart since it was so peaceful.

We had a Great fish fry that night! Everyone chipped in on the cooking and clean up, including me. The happy hour was hilarious too. We all got along so well with each other all week. After all, who could possibly be in a foul mood in this idyllic setting?

On day two I fished with Dave. He had the bizarre and silly notion that walleyes only live in shallow water; too many dumb and misleading fishing shows on TV I guess. I tried to tell him walleyes nearly always prefer deeper water but he would not budge. We never fished deeper than five feet all day! We did not catch much that day. Dave has a poor sense of direction so we got lost on the lake. However, when we drove around a point, we spotted our cabin which surprised him.

On day two Doug fished with Mark and it was a pike bonanza! Doug boated a sixteen-pound pike which Canadians call jackfish. That day he also caught 49 pounds of pike among four fish! He used spoons. By then we all concluded that we really did not need our nightcrawlers. A jig with a bare hook or twister tail worked as well as anything else. We were told by the Northern Outpost sales rep that we would not need any live bait but we did not believe him so we brought a whole flat of nightcrawlers, 500. It turned out that guy was right but we had never experienced this before.

On day three I fished with Ross. It was pure walleye nirvana! We boated about a hundred walleyes and had many doubles. In the evening it rained but the fish still bit well. Fishing in the rain is not as much fun so we always maintained that some liquor in the boat was a saving grace, although not tequila! We only had a half day of rain all week so were blessed.

By the way, we had a family of pine martens living under the cabin's two front steps. We fed them Cheetos all week and they loved it. They were cute and harmless so we adopted them by the end of the week. We wanted to name them but could not tell the difference between the three babies. Apparently, some rodents are cute after all.

The outhouse was twenty feet from the cabin and I could not find it by myself since I could not see or smell it. The guys were very gracious about escorting me there and I was always able to find my way back by listening to them talk in the cabin since the windows were always open. It was a brand new and spacious structure. It was the finest outhouse I ever sat in if there is such a thing. We were proud to use it! One morning Gary slept in. His best friend was ross who decided to wake him up by jostling Gary's shoulder. Gary lunged at Ross and grabbed him by the throat. Ross recoiled in shock and pulled away. It turned out that Gary was a Viet Nam veteran who always reacted this way instinctively when someone touched him during slumber. Not surprisingly, Ross never did that again. Alas, as of this writing, poor Gary is no longer with us due to lung cancer from smoking cigarettes.

One afternoon all three of our boats went into the adjoining lake together in search of bigger fish. The fishing was slow but we noticed a large colony of beavers on the far shore. We drove over there to investigate. There were probably 30-40 of the toothy critters on shore and in shallow water. Apparently, they did not want us around and began slapping their broad tails on the water. This made a VERY loud noise which startled us at first. Soon most of them were doing the same thing. It got to the point that it was an obnoxious sound but captivating. We found ourselves wishing they could slap in unison but they had no natural rhythm whatsoever. They actually surrounded the boat occupied by Ross and Doug and began slapping their tails furiously to frighten us away. They actually splashed water into their boat.

Ross was always full of mischief and often drunk. He decided to chase a few of the water mammals with his little boat. After laughing about this for a little while we told him to knock it off.

None of the beavers were injured since he did not run over any and then we finally left. We had never seen beavers so aggressive before and it was an amazing wildlife experience!

That same night Ross got up to pee around 3 a.m. He noticed very brilliant northern lights which he said were the brightest he ever saw. He wanted to share it so he awakened his childhood friend, Doug. While standing in their undies they marveled at the spectacle until the mosquitos drove them inside. I slept through the whole thing but they talked about it a lot at breakfast. They both used the word glorious and said those heavenly lights seemed closer than any they witnessed previously. We all heard that the aurora borealis were most brilliant the farther north one travels and this was born out on our trip. This was yet another example of the astounding natural beauty of the north Ontario wilderness which Canadians refer to as "the bush." Now we know fully why the northern lights are considered one of the 7 natural wonders of the world.

On day four, I fished with a friend named Mark. It was not as much fun as mark was not an accomplished angler. A good man he was but we had an incident that evening. We drove through the channel into the other little lake. Fishing was slow so we tried to leave around 9 p.m. However, Mark could not locate the channel again. I asked him to drive close to shore and then drive around the lake until he spotted the stream. He did so for a while but to no avail. He kept stopping and was getting more discouraged. At one point he said he was just sick about our predicament. I convinced him to use the same strategy as I knew it had to work eventually. It was getting dusk around 10 o'clock and we were still lost. We heard another motor. We were so relieved that Doug and ross came to rescue us. It turned out the inlet was obscured by a small island which Mark had apparently failed to notice on the way in. We were very happy to get back to our cozy little home.

On our last full day of angling, I was so exhausted I decided to sleep in. Gary fished alone that morning. When I finally got up, I managed to light the gas stove to reheat the breakfast concoction they left on the burner for me. I even made it to the outhouse and back by myself for the first time. As I strolled back to the cabin using my cane, I was hoping I would not accidently stumble into a foraging black bear that would make a quick snack of me: blind man on the half shell! By the way, we were grateful we did not see any bears all week although one screen in the cabin and another in the fish cleaning house were ripped out by bears before we got there.

When the gang came in to clean fish late that afternoon we had a fine time taking photos of their catch of the day. We had 36 walleyes on a long stringer. We tied it up between two birch trees. Each of us stood behind the display for solo pictures as well as three guys with arms locked, hamming it up. That happy photo still hangs on my wall to this day. People comment on it.

The next day was a Saturday and our day of departure. We were told to be on the dock and ready to go at 8 a.m. We got up early and had breakfast and packed up. We were on the dock swatting mosquitos shortly after 8, as requested. Unfortunately, our float plane did not arrive all morning. We were getting a bit worried that maybe they forgot about us and we might have to live on nothing but fish all summer. We also speculated that maybe the plane crashed or simply had mechanical trouble before take-off.

We were bored waiting so to kill time the guys found a length of monofilament lying in a boat and tied it onto my folding white came. They found a hook and tied that on with a piece of rubber worm they also found on the bottom of a boat. I fished off the dock with my white cane and actually caught two small pike. We took photos of me holding up my cane horizontally with a fish still on that hook. Then Gary took me out in the boat, and I caught two walleyes on my white cane!

Not to be outdone, Ross took my cane and jumped into a boat by himself. He drove about fifty feet out and started fishing with it. In about 45 minutes time he had boated and released a limit of six walleyes on my cane. It was true "white cane fishing" and we loved it. We laughed about it.

Finally, about 1:30 p.m. we heard the puddle jumper coming our way. We were delighted and relieved. When it finally taxied up to the dock the pilot said they were fogged in at Armstrong. We had never considered this possibility. The plane already had four guys on it and we loaded up and took off with them. The bush pilot said this plane was a new Cessna that cost two million dollars. When it cleared the tree tops with only eight feet to spare, we all cheered loudly. It was a turbulent flight but we landed okay. We spotted more bears in the ditch on the return trip and a large cow moose by Grand Marais, Minnesota. We arrived at my home town of Cloquet at midnight without incident.

In retrospect, we never caught a walleye bigger than four pounds all week. However, we estimated we boated approximately one thousand walleyes that week so it was hard to complain. We had two possible theories for this bizarre phenomenon. Perhaps the lakes were so choked with walleyes there was not enough feed for them to grow big. However, there was a log book in the cabin and the anglers from the previous week mentioned they had snow one day. Therefore, we surmised that maybe the big female walleyes were still recovering from the recent spawn which causes them to not feed for a week. We forgot to ask the bush pilot about this.

However, Obasi had huge perch. We caught several that were 14 inches long and many 12-13 inchers. We ate some of them and took some home to augment our walleye fillet stash. We agreed that we would not return to Lake Obasi due to no big walleyes but we certainly did not regret going there. Although it was a fantastic and worthwhile angling journey, I soon came down from my fishing high as you shall see shortly.

CHAPTER SEVEN: FISHING THE 2000'S

Although we had the trip of a lifetime on Lake Obasi we never tired of angling so A week later we camped at Agate Bay Lodge on the northeast side of Lake Mille Lacs. This time Doug's 8-year-old son Tyler accompanied us for three days of merriment. We had three mayfly hatches during the three days. There were billions of them in the sky. They covered the tent, the boat and vehicles, not to mention the water. After supper on the picnic table the first night I opened a can of beer and within a minute or two my beer was full of mayflies! They did not taste all that great so I poured it out.

Mayflies usually wreck the fishing since the walleyes are busy gorging on the pesky bugs, feeding on the surface like trout. I only caught two fish all weekend but Doug and Tyler each caught a 25 incher on the Blue Jug. The latter is a mid-lake structure containing a small weed patch. Every time we found that week patch, we caught at least one 6-pound walleye.

Many of the hot spots on Mille lacs have names, some of which are colorful such as the grave yard, the blue jug, spider island, the sliver, the boot, Anderson reef and Indian point. We knew them all well although we did not name them. We even had the GPS coordinates for each of them from our "Walleye Whiffer" lake map. I also had the Minnesota Lakemaps chip in my locator.

Unfortunately, this trip did not end up well. We pulled up to the dock at the resort at the end of our last day. I was carrying the large boat cooler which did not have wheels. At the same time, I was trying to use my white cane which I could not wield well since both hands were full. I went off the side of the dock right on top of the dock pole. I ended up hanging upside down by my pants with my head in very shallow water. I yelled for Doug since I could not get loose and my leg really hurt. He ran over and got my leg unhooked and I fell. He dragged me onto the shore, asking if I was hurt. I replied, "I don't know but my leg hurst." In the meantime, that big cooler actually floated away which surprised us since it was full and heavy. Another boat retrieved it while Doug and his son trailered the boat while I lay there taking stock of myself.

They got me into my van and we drove the block to our campsite. Tyler and I went into the tent to examine my injury. When I took off my ripped pants and showed my thigh to Tyler he gasped and yelled, "Dad, get in here!" Doug checked it out. I lost a lot of skin but very little blood. It certainly hurt but I knew I had to disinfect it. In only my shirt and briefs I walked out to the picnic table. I leaned over it and stretched my leg backward. Doug poured a pint of hydrogen peroxide on the back of my thigh. It only stung a little but sizzled for quite a while. Luckily, I had another pair of pants. Doug told me I was trying to do too much considering the fact that I could not see anything. It healed up okay with the help of my girlfriend though. It turned out this would not be the last time I would fall off a dock but it was the first. Considering I was on hundreds of docks by then I thought I was doing pretty damn good. Onward and upward!

By the way, after that incident I bought a boat cooler on wheels with a pull up handle like a suitcase, which only required one hand to drag, leaving my other hand free for my white cane. I had much more success and safety with this.

We kept lots of beverages of all kinds in that cooler as well as sandwich meat. We always ate lunch in the boat instead of driving to shore to find a cafe or cook lunch on our Coleman stove. We figured it's pretty hard to catch fish on shore, so we always ate in the boat in order to keep our lines in the water. The longer we keep our lines in the water the more we catch or at least have better odds of doing so.

On July 8, 2000 my employer, Fond du Lac Band of Lake Superior Chippewa in Cloquet MN, hired KDK charter fishing boat out of Duluth for me to take two Native teenage boys on charter fishing. I just completed an 8-week anger management program for teenage boys and two of them had perfect attendance. Therefore, the clinic director, Phil Norrgard, paid for three of us for a half day fishing trip.

We went six miles out from Barkers Island in Lake Superior. We fished with down riggers about 100 feet down. These boys had a heyday and limited out on lake trout and one salmon each. The 17-year-old boy even boated a 22-pound laker.

The crew was always looking for the break in water temp. For instance, when the temp changed from 58 to 59 degrees there was usually a school of fish hanging there. This happened several times that day and was new to me.

The boys were very excited and after a while I asked them how they feel. They both replied "great." I retorted, "now doesn't this high feel better than any high from street drubs or alcohol?" They agreed with my point. Captain Dave and his helper did a great job and even clean the catch for the kids. When my girlfriend was driving us home, I put in a Mozart tape for our listening pleasure. The boys asked, "what is a Mozart?"

The very next spring Captain Dave called me at my office and said he would like to hire that 17-year-old Native boy to be his deckhand for the summer. Due to confidentiality, I could not give out the phone number of the boy, but I called his mother and gave Dave's number to call him back. It turned out that this boy, who was now 18, worked all summer getting paid to fish. The boy thought he had died and gone to heaven! I am still grateful to the res, Captain Dave, and Phil Norrgard for this great experience and for enhancing the life of that young man.

In September of 2000 we had another unusual experience on the water. While fishing a small panfish lake near Cloquet we witnessed a bald eagle fly down to the surface and grab a fish out of the water. My boat mates said it looked like a small pike. This is a common sight on the waters of northern Minnesota. However, what made it unique is that another eagle attacked the one with the fish in its talons and there was a mid-air struggle. With both predators flapping their big wings the fish was dropped and got away in the water. The birds separated and took off, not to be seen again that day. We realized that wild animals are always competing with each other for prey so I guess we should not have been surprised.

In January of 2001 Doug, Jeff and I went ice fishing on Lake of the Woods. We had a cabin on shore with Sportsmen Lodge and a day house rental far out on the ice. The bombardier, which is a small bus on tank tracks, took us out every morning and picked us up at dusk. Walleyes never bite on this strange body of water after dark any time of year. This is the only walleye lake we ever fished where they don't bite after dusk. On every other walleye lake we ever fished they bite better after dark.

The first day on the ice we caught a few sauger. The second day was bad. We got skunked and the Vikings lost their playoff game to the Giants 41-0 which we heard on my radio in the shack. Doug was so bummed out he got really drunk in order to drown his sorrows and because he could. On the bombardier ride back to shore there were three women teachers on board who were fishing without any guys which is unusual for ice fishing. When we asked them how they did one giggled, pointing to her friend, "she had the hot hole!" Everyone laughed but we did not dare touch that one.

When we got to our cabin Doug went right to bed at 6 pm. Jeff laid down for a nap. I was not tired and struck out to find the restaurant by myself with just my cane. All I saw was one light, so I headed for it without knowing what it signified. Fortunately, it was the light to the café. A few minutes after being seated and having a beer appetizer, my brother Jeff arrived and we had a nice meal. We never saw Doug again that night. Not sure how we made it back to our 2-bedroom cabin; two blind guys in the dark. By the way, Doug had recently won a pile of money at a casino and paid for our trip. This was unusually generous of him and we knew it would never happen again. We were right.

In late June of 2001 Dave and I fished the Cass Lake area for three days while staying at his mother in law's trailer. Right after I boated a four-pound walleye on a weed patch in Lake Andrusia we noticed the transom of my Smokercraft was separating from the hull on the starboard side! This concerned me greatly since I feared the entire transom might fall off the back and sink to the bottom of that lake. We pulled up to a secluded shore and I took off all my clothes but my undies. I walked around the back of the boat in the water and took off the 15 hp kicker. I handed it over the portside to Dave who laid it on the floor. That finished off our fishing that week.

I decided I needed a new boat so on the way home we stopped at Grand Rapids Marine. After looking at several boats I decided to deal on a 2002 Crestliner Fish Hawk 1750 tiller model. After bartering with the manager, Bob, we settled. I ordered an 80 hp 4 stroke Yamaha since I was unhappy with Mariners. Bob was selling boats for 30 years and said this was the first time he sold a boat to a blind man. I prit near burst with pride and we picked it up a couple of weeks later.

In August of 2001 Jeff, Tyler, Doug, and I piled into my ford van and headed to Grand Rapids, MN to pick up my new glory boat. Doug, Jeff and 9-year-old Tyler made the swap. Tyler felt sad saying goodbye to the boat he practically grew up in and actually kissed it goodbye. When we got to the public access of Pokegama Lake just south of Grand Rapids we discovered we had no anchor. We drove back into town and bought one. After we launched the boat, we drove a ways before we realized we left the food and beverage cooler in my van. Back to the dock again. We did not catch much on that lake but another angler told us to try the adjoining lake, Jay Gould, down by the coal burning power plant. We did so and caught 17 big bluegills.

That evening we started catching walleyes in medium water. Jeff caught the biggest walleye of his life that night on his Red Rhino rod and reel; a four pounder. At about 10 pm the bullheads took over so we knew it was time to depart. We could not find our way in the dark since the lake was new to us. A guy in a nearby boat showed us the way back to the public access. It was not a good start. When we got to the dock Doug and Tyler climbed onto it to fetch my van. I was in the boat holding it to a dock pole. The back of the boat was nowhere near the dock but my blind brother Jeff did not know that. He made the terrible mistake of stepping out of the boat without feeling for the dock with his hand first. He stepped out and went down into the drink! The water was over his head and when he popped up to the surface he yelled "where is the fuckin' dock?" I yelled, "Doug, Jeff fell in the lake! I think he is hurt! Get down here!" Doug raced to the dock and pulled Jeff onto it. By the light of the boat light pole Doug could see Jeff's face was covered with blood! Right then a car load of girls just happened to drive through the access and Doug waved them down. He put Jeff in the back and they took off to the hospital with dispatch. Since they knew where the hospital was and we did not we figured this was the fastest way to get him medical help. No doubt those girls were scared of having a bloody stranger in the back seat.

We loaded up the boat with Tyler crying and shook up. We tore into town but did not know where the hospital was so we stopped at a gas station for directions. A few blocks later we parked at Grand Rapids Hospital Emergency Department parking lot. We checked in and were told Jeff was in surgery. We sat in the waiting room for an hour. Poor little Tyler was still sniffling despite my reassurances that Jeff would not die, and he would be okay. When the nurse guided Jeff to us we took him to my van and laid him on the bench seat in the back while Ty sat on the floor. We were relieved this adventure would soon be over. Boy, were we ever wrong!

By then it was past 1 a.m. and dense fog had set in. As soon as we got out of town, we blew two fuses in the van and had to stop. We unhooked the trailer lights and replace the fuses. Shortly thereafter, Doug slammed on the brakes and yelled, "DEER!" A herd of probably 15 deer were bounding across US Highway 2. We resumed our cruise, asking ourselves what might happen next. A little while later Doug slammed on the brakes once again and yelled, "COWS!" It turned out that a bunch of cows were right in the middle of the now deserted highway! If we were not going slow due to fog, we would have struck one of the big bovines. He counted 14 of them. Doug laid on the horn but to no avail. They did not budge or even seem to notice us. Finally, out of desperation I got out with my folding white cane, ready to chase them off the highway. Apparently, the sound of my van door slamming shut got their attention and they began waddling off our lane of traffic. We finally got to my home in Cloquet just before 3 a.m., exhausted and still in a bit of a daze. We were grateful Tyler and Jeff had fallen asleep.

When we got to my house my girlfriend, Candii ran out and said she had a feeling something bad happened so she waited up for us. When she saw Jeff, she said he looked like a Civil War guy with that big white bandage around his head to cover the 30 stitches in his forehead!

We got poor Jeff out of his soggy clothes and put him to bed. Candi threw them in the dryer and we called it a night. It certainly was a wild and frightening maiden voyage for my new rig and us! As I drifted off to sleep that night, I found myself wondering if this day was a harbinger of things to come.

Not to be scared away a couple of weeks later Tyler, Doug and I went back to jay Gould Lake and camped at Sugar Bay Resort without Jeff. The first day we caught a lot of nice crappies and Tyler hooked and boated the first dogfish of his life, a 5 pounder on a jiggle stick. The next day we only boated baby sunfish, often the size of potato chips. They were way too small to keep but most of them were so aggressive they swallowed the hooks. To remove the hooks, we had to rip their mouths apart so most of them died. However, Doug, always a great one for spotting wildlife, noticed there were two white heads sitting in a large nest in a tree on an island right behind us. I suggested we throw the dead sunnies near the island in hopes to feed those eagles. After throwing about ten of them as close to the island as we could we sat and watched. Sure enough, a few minutes later those two birds swooped down to the water and snatched up a lot of the prey in their talons. They made two swipes each. Then we watched them eating the sunnies in their nest. We thought this was very cool and we were grateful those baby sunnies did not go to waste. They got recycled in nature's way with a little help from their friends.

That summer Ross, Virgil and I went to Lake of the Woods to camp on Oak Island once again. This time we caught more fish and had a better trip. However, one night we fished after dark which was a waste of time. We motored up to the dock and tied up. I crawled out of my boat onto the dock. Somehow, I got turned around and walked off the dock. The upper half of my body landed in my boat and the rest of me went into the water. The guys grabbed me by the back of my belt and hoisted me onto the dock, asking if I was hurt. I was not so they got my clothes bag out of the tent so I could change on the dock. I fell right next to the 12-inch radio antenna. If I had fallen onto it, I might have gotten run through! Another one for the books

Later that summer Doug, Tyler and I went to the Gunflint Trail to camp and fish. Jeff wasn't up for that one. We camped at Gunflint Lodge. We bought our bait at Ugly Baby Bait Shop on the Gunflint Trail which we could not resist due to the comical name. Fishing Gunflint Lake was a bust, so we went to Lake Poplar the next day. We caught lots of eating size walleyes but then the game warden arrived to spoil our fun. He checked our licenses which were good. He checked our life jackets too. We had three adult ones. He gave me a $75. Citation for not having a child's life jacket in the boat. I was sullen that he was being so picky but at least he apologized for his zealousness. he also said this is trout country and few people come there to fish walleyes. Apparently, he was unaware the state record walleye, a 17.5 pounder, was caught three miles away in the Seagull River. We never went back to the Gunflint. The highlight of the weekend was my teaching 9-year-old Tyler how to split logs with an axe safely which he fell in love with.

In January of 2002 Dave, myself, and a youngster named Zach, fished Big Wolf Lake for two days. That little lake is near Cass Lake, Minnesota and Dave had a friend who rented ice houses so we got a freebie with two bunks. I brought my portable shelter with cot and heater. I set up just before dark. It was very windy and there was no snow on the ice. Then I went into the sleeper house to fish with the guys. After a cocktail or two, I went out to get something out of my shanty. Using my cane, I swung it all over the area but could not find my house. I decided I must have gotten turned around when I walked onto the ice. I asked Dave to locate it for me. He could not find it either. It was gone! It blew away! The only thing left was two holes I drilled and my 20 lb. LP tank without an attached hose. Dave finally spotted it at the far end of the lake right up against the shore. He refused to retrieve it in the dark. I could not believe that it blew all the way across the little lake! Too bad there was no snow on the ice.

That night I slept in my van without any heat despite the fact the temp dropped to 15F above. Luckily my heavy sleeping bag was still in my van instead of the shelter on shore. I survived the chilly night. The next morning after a hot breakfast in town, we drove across the lake and tied my ice house to my trailer hitch and towed it slowly back to our rental house. It was still windy so we left it tied up all night while I slept in my van again. Fishing was poor and I was happy to leave that Sunday. We concluded we should have drilled a hole at the end of my portable shelter and put a tied stick crosswise down the hole to stabilize the load. However, we never got the chance to test that idea.

In July of 2002 four of us went back to the English river with two boats. We drove all night to get there and had no trouble at the border crossing. We learned over the years that the middle of the night was the best time to cross over since the agents were so sleepy, they never bothered to search us. They often came out to greet us while yawning. Apparently, we woke them.

After pitching our tents on cemetery island, we began fishing. For the first time we brought walkie talkies with us. That way if one boat was not catching much, they would call the other which was having success. Then we would join them and do better. This worked the other way too which increased our catch. However, Scarrow' Bay was out of range, so we were really cut off there. On our last day Doug caught a 9-pound walleye in that bay. Late in the afternoon Ross called us on the walkie talkie to announce that Dave hooked a big one. Since we were close, we drove over to watch the fun. After a wild battle Dave boated a 17-pound pike on a crawler harness. It bit a hole in his net. Pike fishing was always much better on the English River than Basket Lake.

By the last day our beer and ice were about gone so we had to leave. While crossing into Minnesota the border guards actually checked our fish and measured the fillets. We were legal and this was the only time I ever got searched returning to our home land. By the way, while camping on cemetery island I discovered I had mistakenly brought along two of my girlfriend's panties. I should not have told the guys since they teased me all week about it but it was great fun. It took me a while to live this one down. When I got home Candy told me she put those panties in my duffle bag as a practical joke. You should know I never did wear them on that trip. I just kept wearing the same two pair of my own all week which was fairly gross!

In the summer of 2002 Doug and I fished Lake Mille Lacs on the Malmo sand which is about two miles from shore. We drifted all day and hit the walleye jackpot! I boated 17 and Doug had 14. These are the sizes of my five biggest walleyes that day: 4.75

pounds, 5 pounds, 5.25 pounds, 5.5 pounds and 7.5 pounds! They totaled at 28 pounds on five fish, which averaged to 5.6 pounds each. I got most of them on long line leeches but the biggest one on a long line crawler in 25 feet of water. Unfortunately, they were too big to keep legally so we released all my big ones and kept a few eaters. As far as size of fish this was my best day of walleye fishing to date, including Canadian fishing trips. I should add that by "long line" I mean I fished with an 8-foot snell. Doug would fish with a 10-foot snell which meant he had to stand on the transom tray of my boat even with his arms raised over his head in order to get the fish to the surface. On choppy waters this was a bit hair raisin!

In August of 2002 Doug and I took his son Tyler on his first Canadian fishing trip. By now the boy was ten years old and very excited. Doug always told him he had to be ten to go to Canada even though Doug went there his first time at age nine. We kept that a secret from the boy until much later. We drove all night to get to Basket Lake. A few miles south of Dryden we went around a curve. Doug swerved hard to the right. There was a large cow moose straddling the white lines! We missed the head of the creature by a few inches from the outside mirror. The head of the moose was above the top of my full-size van! Doug estimated it weighed about 800 pounds. Tyler was sitting up front at the time since I was snoozing on the bench seat. He quipped afterwards, "dad, my stomach went into my throat when I saw that moose!" Tyler had never seen a moose before and thought it was some kind of monster.

We got to Basket Lake camp at 4 a.m. and did not want to wake other campers much less the resort owners so we snoozed in the van until dawn. We were very bleary eyes pitching my tent.

We checked in, fried some burgers for breakfast and hit the water.

We caught a lot of walleyes on this trip but no big ones. It stormed every day and we soon tired of being wet. Rainsuits are rarely reliable. At the end of the week we threw the leaky tent in the dumpster and drove home with our limits of fish. Tyler fell in love with Basket Lake and Canada too.

In march of 2003, Doug, Jeff and myself as well as Tyler ice fished Splithand Lake by Grand Rapids, Minnesota. It was a bizarre natural phenomenon that day. The air temperature was 60 but the ice was three feet thick! Fishing was poor but the weather was so nice we stayed all afternoon without a shelter. Near dusk Doug lit up his Coleman gas lanterns and set one of them on the ice, not far from Jeff. Jeff was partying and apparently getting careless, and since he was legally blind, he accidently knocked the lantern right down his own hole! We were unable to retrieve it so packed up and left, laughing all the way. It was never a dull moment when blind guys go fishing, especially two at once.

In June of 2003 I went back to Basket Lake with Dave and his 16-year-old daughter Jasmine. We called this the bear trip. When we got to the resort Dr. Anita, owner, told us it had not rained in six weeks. We assured her it would start soon since we were there. We were right. It rained nearly every day and the tents leaked. Furthermore, I forgot to bring my pound of leeches so had only nightcrawlers for bait and a few minnows we bought at the resort. Due to the drought, there were no berries for the bears to consume so they were in camp all week. We probably saw 10 of them.

One black bear was friendly and came a little closer to our campsite each night when we were frying our catch. He just sat on his fat butt and did a lot of yawning and scratching and snorting. On our last night I was sitting around the campfire having a nightcap at dusk when Yogi, as we named him, strolled close to our campsite. Dave and Jasmine jumped into my van. I just sat there minding my own business. Yogi walked right behind me just 6 feet away, next to the tent. Dave jumped out with his camera and took a quick flash photo of the bruin. He then tried to get one of myself in the foreground and the bear in the background. He snapped the camera but the battery was too weak to flash so it did not turn out. It would have been a great photo for framing but it wasn't meant to be, apparently.

Yogi finally waddled off without further incident. Oddly, I was not that scared since I had a strong feeling he would not attack, or perhaps it was the "bottle of courage."

Later that same night we really messed up. We left my boat bag on the picnic table instead of putting it in my van. The next morning it was nowhere to be found. It contained Cheetos, pretzels and candy bars as well as Jasmine's purse. A resort worker went into the woods to search for it with his big dog. He found it mangled in the woods. The food was eaten and her purse was shredded.

Our misfortune was still not over. When we left that morning Dave decided to take a "short cut." This turned out to be a big mistake. We drove two hours out of our way to Atakokan. At least he admitted he had a poor sense of direction. To top things off, Dave did not tell his daughter that we sometimes have cold rain to fish in so she did not bring enough warm clothing and no waterproof footwear at all. The poor girl was cold and shivering most of the week. I gave her as much of my spare clothing as I could. She never went on another fishing trip with us. I guess she learned her lesson. We did not!

Just two months later Tyler, Doug and I went back to Basket Lake. It was unusually hot. The walleyes would not take leeches all week. We went through hundreds of crawlers. When we ran out of our half flat some Wisconsin guys in a green school bus gave us theirs since they were leaving. While drifting the flats Doug boated, weighed and released a 9.25-pound walleye. We caught lots of 3 pounders all week. It was so hot we had to skinny dip twice a day. We would drop the anchor and jump in. I have a step on the back of my deep V hull so we can pull ourselves back into the boat.

Tyler had never seen a bear in the wild before and really wanted his first sighting. One evening we sat him down next to the tent and told him to watch for a bear crossing the clearing on the way to the fish cleaning house. Sure enough, about a half hour later a small black bear wandered across about 50 feet away. Ty got very excited and yelled, "Dad, a bear!" This made his whole trip he said. Unfortunately, we did not get my camera out in time.

We only had one rain shower all week, when we were on the beach bathing and cleaning fish at the far end of the lake. As usual, we got very good service from resort owner, Dr. Anita North, who was the first woman neurosurgeon in Canada. As of this writing she still runs the place with her able assistant, Loren. They are friends from high school in Dryden, Ontario.

Anita is a fascinating, adventuresome lady who has spent time in such fa flung locales as Antarctica and South America. Can't wait to hear her penguin stories the next time I am at her remote camp!

In March of 2004, Doug, Tyler, and myself fished Red Lake. At that time, it was just a great crappie lake. Walleye fishing was not allowed due to low census of them. We fished out of Buddy Hillmans Resort. We drove out six miles on the ice which was three feet thick. I set up my Frabill Speed Shack and Doug had one too. I set my cot in my shack with the heater on high. Fishing was lousy as we apparently did not set up on a school of crappies. At night the wind came up and it was snowing hard. I went to bed early with the help of some Tennessee antifreeze. During the night the wind ripped my tent and the torn part was flapping loudly all night. It was miserable.

When we got up the next morning, we discovered the van was drifted in and so was the road. We had a bite to eat and packed up. Fortunately, I had my cell phone and finally got a hold of Buddy who showed up 45 minutes later and plowed us out. We were very happy to get off the lake. On the way home I found myself wondering if I would have bad dreams about this one. We vowed not to return to Red Lake until the DNR opened up walleye season again. Sometimes you get the bear and sometimes the bear gets you!

On Memorial weekend of 2004, four of us made the mistake of fishing St. Louis Bay in Duluth, which is the western tip of Lake Superior, the largest freshwater lake on planet Earth. Doug, Tyler and I brought Doug's girlfriend Terri along too. We had a good walleye report from her friend about this water. We fished in just 6 feet of water. It was a bizarre experience. The water was black and we kept snagging trash off the bottom. Then it started raining. After two hours of angling in the rain and boating lots of garbage we gave up and went to look for a hot meal. We concluded that the St. Louis Bay was a former city dump that is now covered with water. We never went back there. Guess we got a bum steer.

At the end of June of 2004, we decided to try a different lake in Ontario for our annual Canadian angling excursion. Someone gave us a tip about Pakashkan Lake near Ignace. We decided to try it even though we knew it meant driving on the miserable Gramm washboard road once again. Terri, Doug and I set out for the lodge on Pakashkan Lake with my boat, van and large cabin tent. It was certainly remote and deep in the bush with terrible roads only wide enough for one vehicle. On the last few miles, the tree tops formed a canopy so we were driving through a tunnel, which we loved since it was so picturesque.

We ended up camping next to some guys from Green Bay, Wisconsin who were pretty friendly. However, on our second night we had just gone to bed when they came off the water after 11 pm. Believe it or not, they started their vehicle to shine its headlights into the woods so they could chop firewood! They kept us up until 2 a.m. so we ended up cursing those cheese heads!

Our first five days of fishing were lousy. We did not know where to find the walleyes so we scouted around. We discovered after five days the fish were crowded into a smaller area of the lake. We had lots of rain too which is common in Ontario due to a high-water table since there are 250,000 lakes in Canada's largest province.

One of the few highlights occurred when we found our way to the far end of the lake to the lodges only outpost cabin. It was very remote and pristine on a small island. We tied up to the little dock and got out to explore. The primitive cabin was open and unoccupied with several bunks. There was a picnic table and fire pit and we wished we had stayed there since we would have that end of the lake by ourselves.

On our last day of fishing, we arose to the sight of a large bald eagle sitting in a tree top right above our tent. It watched us for a while and left a feather in our campsite. Doug spotted it and gave it to me. I took it in the boat with us thinking it might bring us good luck. Sure enough, we hit the jackpot! We stumbled onto a section of the lake that had large numbers of fish, mostly walleyes. On that good weather day, we boated well over a hundred walleyes between noon and 8 pm. We lost count after we got to a hundred. We had several doubles and even a couple of triples, the latter meaning all three of us had fish on at the same time. I caught a six-pound walleye there which was our biggest of the week. A little while later, I hooked something very big so I knew it was not a walleye. It shot from the front of the boat to the back in a split second so I knew it was a big fish, probably esox lucius which is the scientific name for northern pike. I fought it for a while and then it shot straight out from the starboard side of the boat. I held on for dear life, knowing it was probably a wall hanger. My heart was pounding as the brute turned and headed straight for the boat! It shot so fast there was slack in my line despite the fact that I reeled fast and held up the rod over my head. Alas, it was too late as the fish got off the jig and got away. I was bummed out but did not know what I could have done differently to catch the big slimer. We never did see it as it never surfaced, unfortunately. The big ones often get away, as you know!

While sitting around our campfire that last night, we thanked the gift of the eagle feather. We had several delicious fish fries that week and came home with three fish limits of walleyes.

This was not the first time we were blessed by an eagle feather which apparently triggered great fishing. Once when Doug and I were fishing off Ginzer rock on Bear Island of Leech Lake we were getting skunked. Suddenly, Doug saw an eagle fly low over the water right in front of us. It dropped a tail feather on the water! He maneuvered the boat so he could pick it up off the surface. Shortly thereafter, he caught nine walleyes in a row. Although I did not catch anything our day of fishing was salvaged. Once again, we thanked the great spirit eagle for the fish blessing. By the way, I ended up giving that eagle feather to my work supervisor, a Lakota woman, since it was legal for her to own it and illegal for us white folks. She was so thrilled she got a tear in her eye and gave me a major hug! This was very pleasurable for me too since she was very well endowed! YUM!

On July 10, 2004 Doug and I fished Lake Mille Lacs once again. Due to a strong south wind, we put in at Izaty's Resort & Country Club on the south end of the lake. We went to Anderson reef in Cove Bay but caught little. We then decided to fish Montezema point which was a mistake. While cruising at full tilt with my 80 hp Yamaha we bottomed out on an unmarked rock pile! We nearly flew out of the boat and knew we damaged something. I was afraid we might even have a hull breach! We cursed the DNR for not marking that reef with a buoy like they did other spots on the lake. We could not drive off the reef and had to use my boat hook to dislodge the boat, which took some work. When we resumed our cruise, the motor sounded terrible so we pulled up the boat at Izaty's ramp which was deluxe. The skag was dented and the prop was a mess. When we got to my house in Cloquet we installed my spare prop which I always keep in the boat for this very reason. More than once in my fishing excursions we had to pull the boat up to shore, wade into the water to change props on an island somewhere.

In August of 2004, Doug and I went back to Basket Lake Camp in Ontario with his only son Tyler, now age 12. We left Cloquet that morning and on the way out of town went through Hardees drive up window for brunch. Our order was number 13! Just a mile north of town we blew a trailer tire. It pretty much exploded. We got the spare on and went to Junction Tire in Cloquet, Minnesota to buy a new spare. We finally departed town at noon, headed for the border crossing at International Falls. For some reason we neglected to hide the pound of leeches that were in an oxygen bag. Sure enough we got searched and they confiscated our leeches. We were happy they did not levy a fine. We bought a pound of leeches in Fort Francis for $30. US and headed for Dryden, already two hours behind schedule.

We finally got to the resort at dusk and checked in. We pitched our tent in the dark and the mosquitos were terrible. Tyler decided to spray up with what he thought was insect repellent. It did not smell like repellent so we got the flashlight on the can. He sprayed himself with lubricant! We had a good laugh over that one and he said it kept the bugs away anyway. However, we were afraid he might slip right off his cot!

After crawling into our sleeping bags at 10:30 it started raining gently. At 1 a.m. I was awakened by a very strange noise. I lay there in the dark trying to figure out what it was. Very soon I noticed my ears were being dive-bombed by mosquitos. Doug woke up because of them and shone the lantern light around the tent. He exclaimed, "there is a huge hole in the tent right next to your cot!" It was a bear that ripped the hole just a foot away from my head! The hole was big enough to crawl through! Fortunately, I had lots of large safety pins so we pinned up the fabric as best we could. After killing a lot of mosquitos, we finally got back to sleep.

After a Paul Bunyan breakfast we drove the boat to the far end of the lake to our favorite fishing spot. We were catching walleyes left and right including some hefty ones. The rain started up again so we suited up. About an hour later I was feeling very wet. My rain suit jacket was leaking! We drove to shore to clean fish and change clothes. I brought a spare rain suit but it was in the van. I put on a dry shirt and we hit the water. It continued to rain and I was soaked. About mid-afternoon we headed back to camp. To our dismay the tent was flooded! My sleeping bag was wet as well as my pillow. We pitched the tent on a gentle slope and we actually had a small rivulet of water flowing from my end of the tent to the other!

We were in a bad mood but needed to do some brainstorming about whether to go home or stick it out. The forecast was for two more days of rain. After weighing the pros and cons we decided to go home to my house in Cloquet to fish the area lakes. Tyler cried since he did not want to leave. While taking down the tent we noticed that we erected it right next to a big pile of bear scat which we did not see in the dark the night before. No wonder that bear wrecked our tent. This was his way of letting us know we invaded his space. Black bears mark their territory this way. We threw yet another of my tents in the dumpster and drove home.

We commiserated that with all of our modern technology we were amazed that in our high-tech, space-age world no one could apparently manufacture a tent that does not leak after just two weeks of use. I have had many different brands and types of tents with the same result even if the tent is a very expensive one.

We got to my home in Cloquet late that night and slept in the next morning. It rained hard all day so we did not want to fish. We dried out our clothing and sleeping bags and that night played trivial pursuit. At the end of the night Tyler whispered to me, "geez, I never knew my dad was so dumb!"

The next morning, we drove to lake Winnibigoshish, about a hundred miles mostly west. We caught walleyes that day but nothing to write home about. We wanted to fish it again the next day but we did not want to drive all the way back to Cloquet. We decided to look for a cheap motel in nearby Deer River, Minnesota.

As we entered Deer River, we noticed a dumpy looking motel named the Bahrs Motel. It looked a little like the Bates Motel from Alfred Hitchcock's infamous movie, "Psycho" so we thought we better check it out and hoped Norman Bates wasn't working that day!

When we walked in the office door, we got slammed by a very potent stench of cat litter box that apparently had not been cleaned out in ages. We almost gagged and I was afraid little Tyler might faint. The guy at the registration counter had to be over a hundred years old; a true dinosaur who obviously lost his sense of smell. Tips, the fat cat, was lying on the desk and tried to bat my hand away when I proffered the cash for the room. We were a little nervous about entering our motel room. It was a pit with a hole in the ceiling. The sheets on the bed looked like they had not been washed since the crucifixion! Fortunately, we brought our dry sleeping bags in the van and carried them in to sleep in since we did not dare sleep in those sheets. Believe it or not, Doug fried some burgers for us on my Coleman stove in our motel room. Just as we crawled into our sleeping bags, properly lubricated, (us not the bags) a small piece of the ceiling fell on

Doug's head! The next morning, we found silverfish in the shower! Needless to say, we were relieved to check out of the legendary Bahrs Motel. We agreed at least Norman Bates would have kept it cleaner! In more recent years we noticed that dive was leveled; no doubt condemned by the city. Urban renewal.

We decided not to drive the 45 minutes back to Big Winnie so we fished Splithand Lake right by Grand Rapids, which is next to Deer River. The weather was good but the fishing was slow. For some reason we could not discern why several boats crowded around us. We were not catching much so I decided they must have liked the way Doug looked. I knew how to get rid of them. I pulled my harmonica out of my fishing vest and began playing a few folk songs. Sure enough, a few minutes later all the boats but one departed to the far end of the lake. The only boat near us was full of fat women with very short hair. They said they loved my harmonica playing and were disappointed I threw it in the lake. I explained it had some bad notes and was very old. It turned out they had a lot more walleyes than us so we felt a bit sheepish. On top of that, my 80 horse Yamaha motor conked out again. Good thing we had an 8-horse kicker to get us to the dock.

Around supper time we left for Cloquet. I sang "Over the Rainbow" all the way home. When we got home the boys said they never wanted to hear that song again. Our primary recollection of that trip was that we got out-fished by a boat load of dykes. Apparently, we needed to be humbled and, indeed, we were.

We have always maintained that about one out of every four fishing trips come with lots of adversity. This was one of them. We reasoned that since we got that out of the way we should be good for a while.

However, one summer evening I was angling Lake Mille Lacs again; this time with Roger and Ken V. We were anchored over the rocks in Agate Bay which was our favorite reef. There was a little breeze and the water was choppy but the anchor held. I had to pee and then discovered that I had forgotten to bring the obligatory Folgers can in the boat for that purpose. I decided I had to pee over the side of the boat. Since the boat was bouncy, I moved up front where the deck was elevated and decided to get on my knees to pee over the side.

Right in the middle of my stream a big wave slammed against the other side of the boat. Since I was top heavy the motion flipped me over the side, headfirst into the drink with my dick hanging out! When I popped up to the surface Ken yelled, "man overboard!" Since my boat was a deep V, I could not pull myself in so Ken helped me hoist myself on board. I was not injured but a little shook up and my glasses went to the bottom of the lake. I shivered in the cool night air for about an hour. I felt I did not have the right to ask them to leave just because of my foolish mishap so I just toughed it out.

I was grateful when they decided to go to Grand Casino Mille Lacs on the way home for the midnight breakfast special. I sloshed into the café and the waitress commented on my condition. The special was a big breakfast for only $2.99. Since I felt sorry for myself, I treated myself to the biggest steak on the menu which the guys could not understand. That night I learned another important lesson: never take my boat out of the garage without two coffee cans. To this day, I still get teased about this comical event which was not funny at the time. Another one for the books. Still trying to live that one down. Good thing I know how to swim.

In January of 2005, Tyler, now 13, and Doug and I fished Lake Mille Lacs on agate reef. Fishing was terrible. The highlight of the trip occurred when we gassed up in Garrison, MN at a convenience store/station. While waiting for Doug to pay up Tyler was staring at what he thought was a little kid standing outside the station smoking a cigarette. After a minute or two he yelled, "that's not a kid, that is a midget!" He jumped out of the van and ran up to the little person and asked, "are you a midget?" The man said yes and they talked a bit. Then Tyler went inside to find his dad and there was a lady midget cashiering on a high stool! This little couple was managing the business. This was the first time Tyler ever saw a midget and he giggled about it for nearly an hour afterwards. He said it made his whole day that he finally met his first midgets. As you know, 13-year-old boys are a squirrely bunch.

In March of 2005 Doug and I went back to Red Lake for some jumbo crappie fishing. We paid the resort to use their access and plowed road. We set up our portable shelters a few miles out on the ice. Near dusk the slab crappies started feeding. I even caught a couple of big ones on my rattle reel which is unusual for crappies.

That night I decided to sleep in my van so I set my heater in the vehicle on a 2 x 8 plank with the 20 lb. tank outside the side door. The bench in the back folded down to a bed of sorts and I had my heavy sleeping bag. For safety reasons I slept with the side door open and the driver's window open for cross ventilation. I stayed warm and did not get gassed. Doug slept in his tent on a little cot but fished most of the night. We left at noon the next day with 17 crappies weighing between 1.5 and 2.5 pounds. We marveled that we did not get snowed in this time like we usually do on Red. Nevertheless, we got stuck on the ice and three guys from Hutchinson towed us out of the deep snow. When we got to my house in Cloquet I called my new friend Ken who came over to drool over our catch and we had a great fish fry.

In 2005 Ken and I joined a fishing club out of Moose Lake. Every week that summer we fished a different lake with other boats in the club. The first evening it rained so we got skunked on A Prairie Lake by Cromwell. The next Wednesday we fished Island Lake. There was no one on the lake but us the whole time. It turned out we fished the wrong Island Lake. There are three Island Lakes within twenty miles and we did the wrong one which was a bit humiliating. When I called the club manager the next day, he apologized for not being more specific about which Island Lake. At least we caught some pike including one "point fish" from Ken. We fished with the club a couple more times that summer but caught little so we didn't even place.

CHAPTER EIGHT: PASSION IN ONTARIO!

In June of 2005 Dave, Ken S. and I decided to try Pakashkan Lake once more. Although we did not have great luck on previous trips to that water except for the last day of the last trip, Dave and Ken wanted to try it again. However, the day before departure Dave had a serious stroke and was in St. Mary's hospital in Rochester. I called Ken to ask him if he still wanted to go since he would have to do all the driving of the van, and boat as well as clean all the fish. I offered to switch to Mille Lacs for the week since it's so much closer and would save money on gas. He said he still wanted Canada so I agreed. Ken was never afraid of work.

The next morning, we hit the dusty trail. On the north shore of Lake Superior, I called Dave from my van right in his hospital room to tell him we were dedicating the trip to him. He could hardly speak, poor guy. While crossing over at the Pidgeon River border at Grand Portage Minnesota the narcs confiscated our nightcrawlers, claiming there was soil in our bedding. He was just being a dick since Buss bedding never contains soil. One more bad experience at that crossing.

Since we got delayed at the border again, we did not think we could get to the outpost cabin at Pakashkan by dark, so we got a room at Kekebeka Falls Motor Lodge which had AC. It was unusually hot that whole week; 90 degrees!

By noon the next day we finally got to the resort after suffering through the dreaded Graham Road once again. A young woman, named Rosie, was working in the resort office and told us they got a cancellation on cabin 2 and would rent to us at half price. We said yes and checked in. After an afternoon of slow fishing, we had supper and were relaxing on our deck. Rosie came over to visit us. It turned out she was a 19-year-old college student from Thunder Bay who was doing a summer internship at the resort. She was friendly and easy to talk to with a good sense of humor. When it started sprinkling, she said she thought rain was sensuous! Apparently, this made Ken uncomfortable since he was a married man and a bit prudish so he went into the cabin. Oh, I forgot to mention he was also a pastor of a fundamentalist church in Cloquet.

After more sharing and giggling for an hour or two Rosie invited me to join her in her pup tent for some smooching since it was now dark. I said sure! We crawled into her little tent and began smooching. She said she did not like French kissing which was surprising. She was the only woman I ever met who dislike this kind of happiness. Perhaps I simply had bad breath. At any rate, she also told me she was having her period. I was feeling a bit deflated when suddenly she began caressing my crotch! I took off my pants and undies in record time! She started stroking me and gave me a great hand job at which she was quite skillful! Yum!

Afterwards, I was cuddling her in my arms, which I always do, with much gratitude when a man showed up at her tent asking if he could come in. She said no, she was sleeping. After a silent pause of probably one minute, we started giggling. When I asked who that was, she said it was the guy she was with the night before. Yikes! When she walked me back to my cabin at midnight Ken was still up working on his eight rods he brought. I said, "what a resort" and went to bed grinning.

It was so hot in the boat in the daytime Ken and I had to skinny dip twice a day to stay comfortable. Somehow, we ended up fishing in 4 feet of water one afternoon and Ken hooked a big walleye. He got it on the surface, and it looked like a 6 pounder. While trying to net it himself he knocked it off the hook with the net and it escaped. By this time my eyesight was so bad I could not net fish otherwise we would have boated that one. I felt a little guilty.

We caught enough to have a few fish fries that week but the highlight was little Rosie. I invited her over for steak one night and fish the next. She did not have to work evenings so she fished with us two nights in a row. The first night it was hot, but we caught some walleyes on slip bobbers in a spot she knew. It was so hot She and I skinny dipped but Ken jumped in with his undies on. The next night we fished the same spot with her and caught more fish. We caught more walleyes with Rosie that week than without her which we didn't mind too terribly much.

As the week wore on the chemistry between us and our feelings for each other grew stronger. Our last night at the resort Rosie said her period was over and invited me to her little trailer. However, she wanted to wait until late, thinking that the resort manager might not see us sneaking off to her little trailer. It didn't work. As soon as we started walking there came her boss, who simply muttered, "tsk, tsk, tsk. What would your mother say?! Nevertheless, we made sweet, passionate love and came at the same time, which she said was a first for her. About a half hour later we did it again and then I held her until 2 a.m. which I also savored.

When she walked me back to the cabin she quipped, "damn, for an old guy you're not too bad." I told her blind guys always make the best lovers due to our sensitive touch! We laughed all the way to the cabin and even laughed as we kissed good night. However, it was bittersweet since we both knew this was our last night together. I told her I would find her in the morning to say good bye. Just before departing the next morning, I ran back into our cabin to change pants and Rosie was cleaning the cabin. I said, "I hope I didn't forget anything." She replied, "just me."

I very much wanted to take her home with me, but I knew it would never work since she was 19 and I was 52. She said I treated her better than any other guys. I said I hope she never settles for less than the kindness I showed her. It was a sad kiss goodbye.

In retrospect, I never dreamed I would make love in Canada, and it certainly never happened again. We never went back to Pakashkan since I knew it would never be the same without cute little Rosie with the nice figure.

Ken disapproved of my passion with her since he thought it was sinful to have pre-marital sex. I told him the reason we made love is because we were NOT married, thus both available. He pouted all the way home and I was disappointed he judged me.

Nevertheless, we remain friends to this day. He is mellowing as he ages.

In conclusion, we only came home with 5 walleyes and we wrecked both props on unmarked rock reefs. While replacing them with the spares I always carry in the boat Ken got a huge bloodsucker stuck to his leg since we had to change the props in the water. It bled for a long time but he did not turn into a werewolf. Ken paid for half the cost of prop repair later.

Later that summer Doug, his son Tyler and I decided to try a new lake in Ontario named Indian Lake. Unfortunately, Doug brought his grumpy girlfriend Teri along. We had a cabin on that musky lake. It turned out that the high musky population ate up most of the walleyes in the lake which the resort owner confessed to when we checked out. We caught few fish, but Doug boated a 16-pound musky. It smelled so bad that Teri barfed over the side of the boat.

On our fourth day we decided to load up that evening so we could make a hasty getaway early the next morning. Without breakfast we drove to McDonalds in Dryden where we ate. They had a pay phone and Doug called Basket Lake Camp to see if they had a cabin or trailer for one night. They did so we drove there and checked in. We spent that afternoon and the next morning catching big walleyes on our favorite spot. Teri was irritable and moody all week which really put a damper on things and seemed to make the long ride home even longer.

I never could understand how anyone can be in a bad mood on a Canadian fishing trip. When I am on a major angling adventure anywhere, I am flying high on adrenalin the whole time, on top of the world. She also seemed to have an anger problem. I never invited her on another trip. About a year later Doug left her after she threw a cooler at his head.

The next winter Ken and I went ice fishing on Boulder Lake by Duluth. As we drove onto the ice there was a snowdrift in the poorly plowed road on the lake. Ken decided to try to jump it with his little Subaru. I replied, "I don't think cars can jump, Ken." Nevertheless, he gunned it and we rammed right into the drift. We stopped dead in our tracks. Unfortunately, we were not smart enough to bring a shovel or we could have dug ourselves out. We cleared out as much snow as we could with our hands, arms and feet but to no avail. Ken called Triple A and they said it would be two hours before they could get to us. At least his car still ran so we could stay warm. We were blocking the path when a large truck arrived behind us. They were kind enough to tow us out with their chain. Actually, they had no choice since they could not get to the fishing spot at the far end of the lake as long as we were blocking the way.

When we got out, we decided to switch to nearby Island Lake since there was just too much snow on Boulder. As we rounded a curve, we hit a patch of black ice and slid into a shallow ditch, taking out a mailbox in the process! Somehow, we got out by my pushing the front of his car while he gunned it in reverse. When I crawled back into his car I said, "Ken, I wonder if this means we are not supposed to go ice fishing today?" By then it was also getting dark so I suggested we forget about fishing and go to the Buffalo House for an early supper. I was relieved he agreed. We feasted on buffalo prime rib, which was tough, but the tap beer saved the day before we motored back home. I did not catch a walleye through the ice that winter despite several attempts.

At the end of June in 2006 Dave and his friend, Roy, and I tried to go to Basket Lake Camp but the Canadian border agents at International Falls had other ideas. They would not let us into their province since Roy had a reckless driving charge on his record eight years earlier in Minnesota! We could not believe how strict they were being. We cursed them and decided to drive to Baudette, Minnesota to get a cabin. Borderview Lodge had an opening so we took it. That resort was on Zipple Bay of Lake of the Woods which had little structure. We had tough fishing all week and caught little. We didn't really know where to go either. A boat from our resort took pity on us and had way over his limit of fish and gave us one limit. This happened three times that week which was a humbling experience for us. Thanks to that guy who had down riggers on his boat and was using crankbaits we had fish fries and even went home with a few walleyes. We never took Roy with us again as he never told us he had a record.

At the end of July in 2006 Ken and I went to Lake Mille Lacs again. We put in at the Wealthwood public access which is on the north end of the lake. We were truly amazed when we saw thousands of dead tullibees floating on the water. We had no idea what caused this and never saw it before or since. There was a god-awful stench of dead fish but walleyes were feeding on them and minnows were jumping out of the water! It was very hot and the water seemed cloudy and rancid. To make matters worse there was a major mayfly hatch.

When we finally got out to 9-mile flats to slip bobber fish the black thunder clouds rolled in with lightning. We got off the lake just in time and drove home. The best catch of the day was Ken pulling in a rusty minnow bucket which he mistook for a lunker at first.

In late April of 2007 Doug, Tyler and I went to Jay Gould Lake by Grand Rapids once again. We bought our bait at Ben's Bait. Ben said we would not catch any sunfish today. We only had to fish two spots to keep 35 sunfish and five nice crappies, including a 13 incher I boated. We drove back to Cloquet to clean fish and order pizza. No adversity today for a change and even the rain let up when we got to the boat access by the power plant. We never told Ben about our success as we did not want the word to get out and we did not feel the need to rub his nose in it.

I have always wondered how bait shops usually know where the fish are active. We have never once stopped at any bait shop to report our angling success or failure on the way home but apparently some people do. Most guys who run bait shops say they have no time to fish since the business is open seven days a week.

For the walleye opener in 2007, Doug and a bus driver friend of mine named Russ went to Mille Lacs. The weather was good so we were able to boat out to the Boot structure which was several miles away after putting in at Barnacle Bills. Since we had some wind, we drifted with our drift sock out about 20 feet which slowed us down perfectly well. We made many passes and caught walleyes each pass. I had a four fish limit of a 7 pounder, a five pounder and two 17-inch eaters. Doug also had a limit with his biggest measuring at 28 inches. I got all mine on a white floating jig head and leeches. Poor Russ only caught one fish. We noticed his fiberglass rod looked like a pool cue. Twice his leeches got bit in half and he never felt the bite. A grand time was had by all as we noticed most boat were netting fish that day.

We always caught more walleyes on Mille lacs than any other Minnesota lake. However, Mille Lacs walleyes won't take minnows on open water. Not sure why but we never took minnows in my boat for that very reason. This was the only lake I ever fished where walleyes won't take hooked minnows; a totally unique body of water. Of course, they will feed on minnows in the winter since that is about the only food available to them.

At the end of June of 2007, we had a dangerous experience on Mille Lacs. We checked into our cabin at Fishers Resort which is in the northeast corner of the lake. The resort operator told us on the phone the cabin had two beds and a rollaway. There was no rollaway and they did not have one so poor Ken slept on the floor the first night. After that he slept in my van since the bench seat folded down into a bed.

The first day was good although hot. We caught some nice walleyes on the Blue Jug in the wind. Dave caught a 7 pounder on 9-mile flats and then started getting seasick, so we took the wuss to shore. Since it was so hot and it was happy hour Ken and I decided to take a swim. This time we even wore trunks!

We sat in water up to our necks and drank a couple of beers which fortified us for supper. That evening Ken and I slip bobbered the rock reef in agate Bay but without much luck.

The next morning Dave still felt queasy so he did not want to get in the boat. Doug showed up at 9, as planned. We did not know what was in store for us that fateful day. There was a 15-mph wind which on Mille Lacs generates 3-foot waves, so we drove the van and trailer to the opposite corner of the lake to the Cove Bay public access which was full of rock hazards.

We started out at Sloppy Joes structure but caught little so when the wind died, we shot out to 9-mile flats. There were fish all over the screen of the locator and we were catching them. I boated a 7 pounder on a gold spinner and jumbo leech.

Suddenly, under a clear blue sky, the wind kicked up heavily! Within 10 minutes the wind went from 10 mph to at least 30! Even quicker the waves quadrupled in size! They got to 5 or 6 feet high! We were trapped 6 miles from the nearest shore! We reeled up and put on our rain suits and life jackets. We had to move slowly since the waves were so big. Several times big waves slammed over the starboard side and pounded the floor of my boat! I had never seen this before and was frightened as were Ken and Doug.

Doug handled the boat as well as anyone could and after 90 minutes of agony, we finally reached calmer waters. Unfortunately, we were also lost. This is the only time Doug ever got lost on Mille Lacs but we knew we were nowhere near

Cove Bay or Agate Bay but somewhere in between. We motored into what turned out to be Waukon Bay and docked at a resort called Fuzzies on the Bay. We went into the bar and learned that we were 8 miles from Cove Bay where my van and trailer were parked. We had no way to get there so the guys were about to hitch hike when a cocktail waitress named Susie offered to give Doug and Ken a lift since she was getting off work right then and it was on her way. They took off in her trashy car which only had room for two passengers, leaving me at the bar. I quickly soaked down two bourbon Manhattans to calm my shaky nerves. When I told the old bartender what we just went through he said we were extremely lucky to be alive. I nearly staggered outside to wait at a picnic table. About 20 minutes later the boys arrived with my rig. While pulling the boat onto my trailer we realized we forgot to switch on the bilge pump while out on the lake! A dumb mistake; an oversight. They switched it on and the stream was shooting out the starboard bow while I was sitting on the dock with my feet dangling off the side. As the boat moved past me the water jet soaked my crotch which the guys saw. We had a good laugh which we really needed at that point. My crotch was soaked and I looked like I wet my pants but I did not care. I was just happy to be alive and back on terra firma.

We must have drained forty gallons of water out of the boat which took 20 minutes. When we got back to our cabin and told Dave what happened he was so grateful he stayed on shore. Doug had only planned to fish one day so took off. We cooked supper but had no appetite for more fishing that night so we got drunk and talked it out thoroughly until we finally started laughing. Catharsis!

The next day the wind shifted out of the northwest so we drove to Garrison, MN and launched at the public access. We discovered we only had two life jackets. Either Dave, Ken or Doug had put one in the cabin the night before and we left it there. No one took responsibility for it and we bought one at the local bait shop and hit the water. It was a tough day of fishing since we were wind-restricted to a small area and the fish simply would not bite. It was a long boring day, and we boated no fish. We started to wonder if the lake would ever calm down. At least we weren't at work, we said to comfort ourselves which did not help much.

On our next day of fishing, we hit the water early since the wind finally let up. We raced out to 7-mile mud flats and caught fish from noon until early evening. We finally had our first fish fry that night with baked beans and had cocktails around our only campfire of the week. The next morning, we checked out and Dave headed south to Lanesboro while Ken and I fished that Friday. We fished on 9 mile again and caught nice walleyes. We went home to Cloquet that night with limits of walleyes. We were glad to be safe at home and in our own cozy beds. All in all, it was another trip to remember in our old age which just happens to be now as I write this in 2023.

Late in July of 2007, Doug, Tyler, now age 15, and I pitched our cabin tent at Mille Lacs Kathio State Park which is just west of the water a mile or two. We had a large, secluded and wooded campsite. We camped across the dirt road from two lesbians. Tyler got a kick out of watching them kiss which they did frequently. They were obviously in love. The temps that week ranged from 90-95. When we scheduled our vacation time for that week, we had no idea it would be so hot, but we decided to tough it out like real he-men anyway, LOL.

With this big water one has to pay favor to the winds in order to stay on the lake. We put in at cove Bay which is the southwest corner since the winds were from that angle. It was a tough and sweaty day of fishing. We were shocked we caught a few stinky bullheads as we did not know they inhabited these waters.

The next morning, we boated four walleyes over 20 inches but had to release them according to the stringent laws. Tyler got none but as we were backtrolling in Garrison Bay he got the thrill of the week. He was casting a large Bulldog lure that probably weighed a pound. Suddenly he had a major follow. Just two feet below the surface was a four-foot-long fish! It had to be a musky but maybe a pike. In all the years I have fished Mille Lacs I have never caught a single pike on open water or through the ice. Doug told him to pull a figure 8 with the lure which did not work. Seconds later the fish flared its gills and dove out of sight.

We worked that 8-foot-deep spot for a good while but to no avail. Poor Ty was disappointed and was shaking for a good while after the excitement. In retrospect, I wish I had the presence of mind to tell him to smack the lure right into the fish's nose so it would have to attack it to defend itself! Alas, we missed the biggest fish of the year. Doug is 6 feet 2 inches tall and that fish was as big as his leg. The rest of that day we could not get it out of our minds, but it was so hot we had to skinny-dip four times a day to stay comfortable. Due to the heat, there were very few boats on the water. Most people had sense enough to stay home in air-conditioned comfort but not us.

That night around the campfire there were four large owls behind our tent. They were sitting in each their own tree. They were hooting like crazy! It was very loud and eerie and at times they screamed like banshees! It was another great natural wonder in our beautiful outdoors. As soon as Tyler and I got in the tent we heard the unmistakable sound of a large critter walking through the brush. Tyler got scared and zipped up the screen window on his end of the tent, as if that would help. We all figured it was a bear but suddenly we heard that chittering call that could only be made by a raccoon. Doug and I laughed that it was only a noisy coon. I told Tyler we will be safe tonight since if there were bears or wolves in the area that coon would have been a lot quieter. That raccoon obviously did not have a care in the world. Indeed, we were safe that night and all week.

By the way, we got a big discount on camping fees in that state park due to my blindness. I had my Affidavit of Blindness with me but once the park attendant saw my white cane he did not ask for more proof. The discount amounted to about 40% which was kind of the state. They do this to encourage people with disabilities to use our natural resources.

The next day we fished the north end. Although we caught no walleyes that day, we found a school of nice smallmouth bass. We boated four that were over 3 pounds, even with slip bobbers! On the third day we drove up to lake Emily and got 24 keeper sunnies to fillet for supper. Unfortunately, my anchor broke off in the little river in 6 feet of water. I stripped and jumped in, determined to retrieve the rubber coated twenty pounder. I dove to the bottom many times but could not feel it so gave up. It must have sunk in the mud right away.

On the fourth day we drove to Lake Trellippe again, one of our favorite little lakes for panfish. In the afternoon we could see a major black storm cloud coming our way so we headed for the dock. We tied up the boat with heavy line on the front and back rings. We jumped into the van just in time. We spent the next two hours sitting in the hot, muggy van, wondering why we left the beverages in the boat. We finally got back on the water but the fish were shut off; no doubt scared off by the numerous loud cracks of thunder. However, we finally had our first fish fry that night.

The last day we fished Lake Washburn. The fishing was slow but the girl watching was great, which Doug and Tyler really enjoyed. On the way home we ate supper at the Bungalow Cafe in Emily which we never knew existed after all our trips to that area. I bought steaks for the three of us which I always do on the last night of our weeklong excursions.

In late June of 2008, Dave and I drove to Basket Lake Camp again, just the two of us. I thought he was fully recovered from his stroke from three years earlier but I was mistaken, as you shall see. Dave got confused about the location of our most productive honey hole and simply would not go there. I kept telling him over and over again that if he can't see the sandy beach, we are not on Gull rock. He insisted that we were. I told him Gull rock does not have trees on it. He said they grew up since we were last here. We caught few walleyes all week since he wouldn't go to our best spots. It didn't help that he has a poor sense of direction even before his stroke.

One afternoon I finally caught a four-pound walleye in an unfamiliar spot. He got a little mad, he resented me for that. We boated a few fish and managed to have a fish fry. In fact, on our last evening I proposed we have a fish fry with one of my eater walleyes and one of his smaller pike. I thought this was a very fair idea. Dave went ballistic! He yelled and screamed for 30-40 minutes over nothing. I told him he was out of line and over reacting which only made him angrier. I am a career psychologist and after a while I started feeling like I was in a therapy session with a client with a severe anger problem.

When he finally wound down, I said the hell with a fish fry. I made myself a cold sandwich and went to bed early. I slept in my tent all week and Dave slept in my van all week since he is terrified of bears. Just as I was drifting off to sleep around 10:30 I heard the loud crash of the steel door on the bear live trap about a hundred feet from me. At the resort owners request, the Ontario Ministry of Natural Resources parked a live bear cage trap on wheels to remove the pesky bears one at a time. That poor bear went ballistic just like Dave! It roared, screamed and growled loudly for at least a half hour. I had never heard anything like this and it was amazing to listen to. Dave did not stir and I finally went back to sleep wondering which one was the angriest, Dave or that bear. The bear had reason to be livid; Dave did not. It was an angry night and I felt bad but finally got to sleep.

The next morning after breakfast David and I sauntered down to look at the bruin. It was lying on the floor of the cage looking at us. Dave said it looked like a whipped pup. We packed up our gear and tent since that was our scheduled departure date anyway. As we were leaving the game warden arrived with a big truck. We watched as he hooked up the cage on wheels. We asked him what he would do with the critter and he told us about their policy with invading black bears. He said he would drive 20 miles north to release the beast. He told us he would stand on top of the cage with a real sidearm and a paint ball gun in his other hand. When he rolled up the cage door and it ran out, he shoots the bear on the butt with a yellow paint ball to mark it. This way they know if it is the same bear coming back. In that eventuality he then drives the bear 40 miles north for the same release. When we asked if he ever had to kill one of the captives, he replied no.

It was a long drive home as Dave decided to take a short cut which turned out to be a long cut again. It gave me plenty of time to think about what happened the night before with his tantrum. He never mentioned it all the way home and neither did I. I decided at that point that I could never be his friend again but did not share this with him yet. By the way, when he left my house that night, I discovered he stole most of my fish fillets. The next day he called and I told him he had a serious anger problem and I am ending our friendship since I don't deserve to be treated that way. Yes, I know that stroke probably contributed to his short fuse but I do not need or deserve abuse of any kind. He and I had no further contact for ten years when I wandered into his windy Mesa shop in Lanesboro with a friend.

We never renewed our erstwhile friendship and never will. He is still best friends with my brother Jeff, however. This was a difficult decision for me since I don't like to hurt anyone's feelings but there are times when we must protect ourselves and put ourselves first.

Just three days later, July 3, the 3 amigos (Doug, Tyler and I) returned to Lake Mille Lacs by way of Kathio State Park. The first day of fishing was slow; only caught two 25-inch walleyes and no eaters for our frying pan. The next day I woke up sick and had to go to a clinic in Onamia, MN where a Physician's Assistant gave me antibiotics for my lung infection. I definitely did not feel like fishing but the prospect of spending the day alone in a super-hot tent was even worse than the idea of being in a boat all day. I slept in my boat the whole day while the guys fished. The next day I felt somewhat better but there were 30 mph winds so we pan fished nearby little Shakopee Lake and did well.

The grand finale of this trip occurred on the fourth of July. The weather was perfect, so we spent the day zipping back and forth between 7-mile flats and 9 mile. Right about suppertime we anchored on the edge of 9 mile and stayed until midnight. We boated eight walleyes, all over 4 pounds. At about 10 pm the guys could see fireworks displays on four sides of the lake. It was so cool. Furthermore, for the first time ever we brought my Coleman stove and a saucepan in the boat. We boiled up brats and ate them on buns with Gray Poupon and lots of beer. It was an awesome finish to another great fishing adventure.

On August 13, 2008, Doug and I angled the west basin of Island Lake, the one just outside of Duluth. It was a beautiful but lopsided day. Doug boated eight walleyes and I got skunked again. We tried several lures but they would only take hatchet harnesses, sometimes called Dakota harnesses. These spinner blades have a V shape which vibrates differently than an Indiana blade or Colorado blade; very effective for walleyes but hard to find especially the ones with three hooks which we always prefer. We get more hooksets with the three hook harnesses than the two hookers.

That night Doug fried up walleyes for supper while I grilled a T-bone steak on my gas grill in Cloquet. We always said it's hard to beat steak, fresh fish and ice-cold beer for supper. We had no adversity today and fishing success, for him anyway. Long ago I gave up getting bummed out when I get skunked on the water. Always a happy camper angler. Even a bad day of fishing is better than a good day at work, right?

On October 4, 2008, Roger and Mike drove up from St. Cloud so we could celebrate Mike's birthday on the water as well as mine. We went to Island Lake and had a tough time at first despite beautiful fall weather. Roger backed my trailer off the side of the ramp which he was embarrassed about. After a while he managed to get it back on the ramp and launched. When we got out on the lake, he could not get my 8-horse kicker started. I said to let me try it. I discovered he had not hooked up the gas line! I said with a little sarcasm, "Look, you guys, these motors run on gasoline so if you don't have the gas line hooked up, they will never start." Then, to rub it in a little more, I asked, "Roger, have you ever started an outboard motor before?" He got indignant at that point since he grew up in boats around

Alexandria. I connected the gas line for him. Then I noticed he had the motor shifted into forward instead of neutral. I told him "it won't start unless it's in neutral, Roger." His reply was anatomically impossible.

We had a good day otherwise. We were catching walleyes backtrolling with minnows and also anchored with slip bobbers. A guy on the water caught so many walleyes he was over his limit and ran out of minnows. He gave us eight eater walleyes for a dozen minnows! We definitely got the better end of that deal. We came home with 18 walleyes, which was the legal limit for three guys on that lake, as well as five jumbo perch. Two of them weighed a pound each, plus the occasional bass which we released. We had another great fish fry that night and a birthday celebration for Mike, his 60th. They left the next day with fillets.

Parenthetically, Roger fished with three lines all day while bobber fishing. He has always done this and has never been caught by game wardens. Many times, while anchored for panfish he used five lines at once. We never could figure out how he never got busted. We would have, for certain so we never did it.

Doug, Tyler and I spent New Years of 2008 on Red Lake in northwest Minnesota. We had a very nice sleeper house we rented from Pat Foster of Club Red Resort. The ice was 17 inches thick so our house was 6 miles out on the ice. There was a lot of snow on the ice but we managed to drive my old Ford van without getting stuck. The first night the mercury hit 32 below without windchill. My van would not start but Mr. Foster,

who cussed like a sailor, drove out to give us a jump. We had
great fishing for walleyes, good food and spirits. We caught 30
eater walleyes in 48 hours which is very good for ice fishing. We
kept our limits. Tyler reeled in a 34-inch northern pike that only
weighed 6 pounds. It looked like an eel. Must have had anorexia
nervosa. Another grand time was had by all with only a little
adversity.

We loved Red Lake and nearly always did well on the ice
especially with rattle reels. The latter is the perfect way for a
blind person to fish since I don't need to see the bobber. I
always loved rattle reeling. My technique with these noisy reels,
which are nailed to the wall, is to let the fish pull out the line as
much as it wants. When the walleye stops pulling out the line
that nearly always means it is stopping to swallow the minnow.
As soon as it starts up again, I set the hook and hoist it in. This
works about 85% of the time. The other 15% there is nothing
but a bare hook when setting it; waited too long.

Late June of 2009, Doug, Tyler and I decided to do something
new for us. We fished Red Lake on open water. We pitched our
big tent at Big Bog State Park. The first day of angling was way
too windy for a bowl-shaped lake like Red. The winds were at
least 30 mph and the lake had big rollers on it with major
whitecaps. We trailered the boat down to Lake Rabideau south
of Blackduck, Minnesota. It was quiet that day on this lake since
it was down in a valley. The nice sunny weather produced only
two walleyes but 20 keeper sunfish. It was great to have a fish
fry on our first day of fishing.

On the second day Red lake was still too rough to fish so we fished the Tamarack River which flows into Red. Doug caught four walleyes that day but Tyler and I boated nothing but sheephead all day. Since we don't believe in releasing rough fish alive, we dispatched probably forty of them with my miniature crow bar which made Doug mad although I don't know why. We fed eagles, hawks and seagulls that day so they did not go to waste: natural recycling. Rough fish eat food that should feed gamefish.

The next day the water was calm so we fished Upper Red Lake. We never boated a fish all day. When we talked to other anglers about this, they claimed that the high winds stirred up the sediment which made the water so murky the fish could not find the bait. We never saw anyone else catch fish that day either. Back at camp a guy said it usually took two days for the reddish sediment to settle. We never heard of this before but suspected it was true. We gave up on Red and the next day went back to Rabideau without any fishing success. The next morning, we packed up and left a day early. We drove down to Bowstring Lake near Deer River. It was a beautiful day but we used a crappy public access without a dock. We only caught four walleyes but had a nice day on the water.

By the way, we never went back to Red Lake to fish open water. Furthermore, we did not like Big Bog State Park; poorly designed. We were practically camping on top of our neighbors since the campsite were so close to each other. We could hear every word of our neighbor's conversation and they could hear all of ours too. The only good thing about this park is that we were allowed to pull up my boat on shore and tie it to a big tree right behind our tent; the epitome of convenience. I would not recommend Big Bog State Park to anyone unless they have changed it since then.

In September of 2009 I took another week of vacation time so Ken and I could fish some lakes in the Cloquet/Grand Rapids area. That summer I was dating a hot, little blond named Chris. I thought things were going well between us and I was in love with her. Apparently, I was mistaken. On my last day of work, she sent me a "Dear John" email at my office. I felt like shit and could not function on the job that day. When I asked her why she said she wanted to date a local guy since she lived in Ashland, Wisconsin. I am sure I was in more pain that day than my clients.

I decided to follow through with my fishing plans anyway even though my heart wasn't into it. On the way to the lake the next day I was crying in the van. Ken was supportive. A couple of days later we went to Bostring Lake by Deer River, MN. I was still feeling lots of emotional pain in the boat. As a psychologist I sometimes used the "empty chair technique" with clients in order for them to express their unpleasant feelings verbally so I decided to try it in the boat. I told Ken I might get loud and asked him to drive the boat where no one was nearby since I would be yelling. He did so and then I imagined Chris was perched in the front of the boat. I was getting a little worked up verbalizing my agony and finally yelled as loud as I could, "I hate you!" Immediately thereafter I heard a man's voice off to the right. He asked, "well, do you want me to leave?"

I asked Ken why he stopped within earshot of that angler and he replied that he did not know I was going to yell that loud. I said, "let's get the hell out of here!" He fired up the 80 horse and we drove to the farthest end of the lake. I certainly felt like a major heel and probably gave the poor guy a complex of some sort! That procedure did not help anyway; it just took time to heal. I am still trying to live that one down as Ken would not let me hear the end of it, LOL. I think I should get the Nobel Prize for publicly humiliating myself. One more thing that would only happen to a blind guy.

We hardly caught any fish that week. On top of that, the 8-horse kicker conked out, so we spent all our time anchored for slip bobbing. On the way home we got another flat tire on the trailer; always the starboard side. When we got back to Cloquet we took the motor to Gene's Marine. It turned out the motor had no oil but was full of water. It was a cheap fix. All in all, it was a trip to forget and I was actually glad it was over. What a way to end up another fantastic decade of angling adventures! That decade started out with a heavenly fly-in trip and ended up in ignominy.

CHAPTER NINE: FISHING THE 2010'S

By this time, I had lost all my vision. I only had light perception left. However, I just kept plugging away with my fishing and my job. It never occurred to me to quit although it was getting more difficult with each passing year since my loss of eyesight is progressive.

In February of 2010, Ken and my dentist, Dr. John C, went fishing on nearby Hay Lake. It was supposed to be a good crappie lake. We drove my old, rusty Ford van onto the ice which had deep snow. Of course, we got stuck close to shore. Even with a shovel we could not break loose. So we called Cars Towing out of Cloquet. They arrived an hour later and he said he was not allowed to drive on any lake since tow trucks are very heavy. However, he had a 100-foot-long chain which barely reached my vehicle. He pulled us out, thanks to Triple A.

We decided to try it again, this time on foot. I was dragging my Clam 5600 ice shelter through knee deep snow. This shelter is not streamlined at all and it was very arduous to drag it. Soon I was dizzy and panting and my heart was pounding so I stopped. The other guys had a smaller shelter and they were way ahead of me. When we got our houses erected, we realized we only had one heater for two houses.

We laughed about this and rotated the heater every 30 minutes since our shacks were withing two feet of each other. Although fishing was lousy, we had lots of laughs and some sandwiches. Dr. John had lots of comical stories including about his dental work with patients. I was secretly relieved he did not bring his dental drill in his tackle box! By the way, he said my rusty old van should be pushed off a cliff. I agreed.

In the spring of 2010, my brother Bill decided to sell his van; a Ford E150 XLT window van with a Triton V8 engine. I bought it at a good price and he delivered it from Rochester to Cloquet with his daughter trailing him in her sedan to bring him back home. I took them out to lunch for their efforts.

With the Triton engine we never overheated even when pulling my boat heavily loaded and running the AC on high. This was my third Ford E150 van and I was delighted it was my first one built in the 21st century. It only had 72,000 miles and was in mint condition. The guys said it drove like a Cadillac so we named it the glory van. Ever since then every time we take it fishing, I yell out the passenger window: "THIS VAN IS BOUND FOR GLORY!" I love my fancy van and still have it. I have very little trouble with it. It has since seen some wonderful fishing adventures and a few not so great.

On May Day of 2010 Ken, Doug and I drove to Jay Gould Lake again to fish by the coal burning power plant which is always pumping warm water into the lake. This draws in the fish since that water warms up sooner than the rest of the lake. We fished in 7 feet of water but only two feet down since the sunfish were suspending all afternoon. We sat through three showers but we kept 54 fish. This was back when the limit was 20 per man. We went through two boxes of waxworms (aren't they the same as maggots?) and a dozen crawlers. They would not touch minnows except for Doug's one large crappie. This fishing success was an oddity since we rarely ever caught sunnies in the rain. They prefer sunshine, hence the name.

When fishing Jay Gould we always had to put up with coal trains barreling across the trestle over the water. This never seemed to bother the fish. We surmised that they were used to it. A few of the bluegills were pounders so we agreed to come back every spring.

The Minnesota walleye opener in 2010 was on May 15. Doug, Tyler and I got to Fishers Resort on the northeast edge of Lake Mille Lacs. We arrived at 8 a.m. on a beautiful morning. There was chaos at the access and people were yelling at each other.

We could not figure out what they were upset about but we managed to launch after only a 30-minute wait which we thought was pretty good since this lake is very popular for opening day. I could never understand why some anglers get stressed out over launching and loading their boat. It's just not that hard unless the waves and wind are high and they were not on that beautiful morning.

At any rate, since the water was calm, we shot out to the Boot for starters. We popped two eaters right away and tossed them in my live well. Then the wind died completely and the fish shut off until evening. We even tried the mud flats while backtrolling and slip bobbering but to no avail. Very few boats were netting fish as Doug is always watching others for clues of hot spots. Unfortunately, my 8 horse Yamaha would not troll down as usual so we were moving too fast for the lazy walleyes. We got out the owner's manual and, surprisingly, Doug was able to turn down the idle. He is not very mechanical either so I told him I was proud of him for getting this done.

At 7 pm we set up on the outside of the Agate Bay rock reef in 14 feet of water. We live welled a few more eater walleyes. Poor Tyler did not catch his first fish until dusk. Between 9 and the 10 pm curfew we all filled out on keepers with lighted slip bobbers and leeches. Everybody was netting fish in our area. It was pretty much fun!

We drove home to loud Moody Blues music on my stereo, very happy we had a great day. We cruised past dead skunks six times that night which was a new record for us and a smelly ride, indeed! However, we had 12 keeper walleyes ranging between 13 and 18 inches. Doug cleaned fish until 1 a.m. Although Tyler was 18 by this time, he never wanted to learn how to fillet fish. However, the next morning we had a bleary-eyed fish fry in my Cloquet home before they departed. This was one of the better fishing openers we had. It was odd that we had a little sunburn since most opening days in Minnesota came with crappy weather. We had a lot of fun even though our biggest walleye was only 21 inches. By opening weekend, the big female fish usually had not recovered from the spawn so they were very hard to come by. As you know, male walleyes rarely get bigger than five pounds.

Late in June of 2010 Doug and I went to Basket Lake Camp again. This time we left Tyler at home. He got into a little trouble and we knew the Canadian border agents would not let him across into Ontario since they are so strict. He was very bummed about this but he knew he brought it on himself.

I always had reservations about going with only one guy but Doug was fine with doing most of the work. After all, he has lots of energy and at least I was providing the van, boat and tent as well as washing all our dishes at the water pump. Besides, with only two guys in an 18-foot boat we had lots of room which was a luxury. My boat has no console to get in the way.

We had no trouble crossing over at International Falls and got to Basket Lake Camp at 4 pm. Dr. Anita told us her mom Olga North died a month earlier of old age. We gave her hugs and our condolences. Dr. Anita took the summer off from her medical practice to run the resort. It was a hot day and we worked up a nasty sweat trying to erect my new tent which was a weird one. Doug isn't able to read diagrams and I was no help. After two hours and an argument we finally got it up. By then we were very thirsty so we had beers and burgers. Then we launched the boat to prepare for early departure the next morning. Unfortunately, mother nature had other plans for us.

That night a torrential storm rolled in with heavy rain and high winds. When Doug awakened at dawn, he saw deep pools of water on both sides of the center pole of my tent. He was afraid the tent would collapse. I woke to the sound of him pushing on the underside of the water pockets to drain it away. When he did the one on my side of the tent somehow water came in through the screen window, which was tied up but still soaked my sleeping bag. There was a lot of water on the floor too so we were very glad we were on cots. We finally got up although it was still drizzling. Doug cooked breakfast for us on my Coleman stove in the back of my van. We ate breakfast in the drizzle while wearing rain suits. Our pancakes were a little soggy but we did not care since it was hot food with coffee that really hit the spot.

After I washed the dishes, we sat in the van waiting for the rain to let up. It never did. Doug wanted to stay in the van and drink all day but I scolded him with the reminder that we have fished very well in the rain many times. He relented and we embarked at noon, still raining.

When we finally got out to our favorite spot, we hit the fishing jackpot! We drifted the area and caught dozens of walleyes. I boated a pair of 25 inchers and a 26 incher. Doug got a 27 incher and a pair of 24's. We caught many over the 20-inch mark. We could only catch two eaters to keep for supper. We quickly discovered that green worked best in the rain. I used a crawler harness with a green Indiana spinner blade and Doug got his on a one hook green spinner and leeches. Green/chartreuse usually works best in the rain for both walleyes and pike. However, we rarely fished for pike on basket Lake since the pike fishing was usually average and the walleye fishing was excellent.

Although we were soaked, we had a great day on the water, catching 40 walleyes. The rain finally stopped as soon as we arrived at the dock. We had a nice fish fry with very fresh walleyes and baked beans. Since everything was wet, we could not have a campfire that night so went to bed early. By the way, my Colman stove malfunctioned all week but Doug brought his as a backup which saved the day.

The next day, Monday, was cold and cloudy but we caught lots of walleyes out at the far end of the lake on three different structures, usually with spinners. On Tuesday, the weather was finally improving and we boated nice fish on our best spots. However, we could not get any eaters for supper so we went to a small bay and got four to eat. I got lots of walleyes over 19 inches and Doug only a few. He was jealous so I had to rub it in, as usual.

On Thursday I got a five-pound walleye off the bottom in 35 feet of water on a half-ounce white jig and leech. It was great fun to fight it up off the bottom from that depth. There was a little wind too which made the pull even stronger. We went back to the little bay in the afternoon to get some eaters.

At this point I already had my four limit of fish to take home, all about 17.5 inches since the size limit was 18.1 inches. Doug decided to wait until our last day of fishing to garner his homer limit. This turned out to be a mistake since the next day the fish shut off completely at 1 pm. We fished until late afternoon without a bite which is unusual on Basket. We were hoping to have a fish fry that night but we passed so he could take home his limit of fillets. We had leftovers our last night in camp. He said he learned his lesson and would never again wait until the last day of fishing to keep his catch. If he tries it, I will remind him.

We got across the border with no difficulty. U.S. border agents are not as strict as those Canadians. Believe it or not, we had no mosquitos until the last day! We were shocked as there is usually swarms of them around our campsite. However, the no see-ums were out in force. Doug is allergic to this insect bite and by the end of the week of every Canadian trip he has oozing welts from them except when we stay in a cabin. We were also pleased there were no black bears in camp which was unusual.

We fished six days in a row until we finally got our fill of it. We get so spoiled on Ontario fishing we don't usually bother to fish in Minnesota again for a whole month after returning.

On October 9, 2010 Roger and Mike and I stormed Boulder Lake by Duluth for walleye fishing. We never caught a walleye all day but hit a crappie bonanza! While drifting the channel with 1/8-ounce green fireball jighead and fathead minnows, we got 14 crappies over 1.5 pounds each! My biggest was 2.5 pounds and the biggest of the day was 2.75 pounds by Roger who fished with 3 lines all day, as usual. The highlight of the day for me was boating a jumbo perch that clocked out at 2 pounds 4 ounces, by far the biggest of my life. Perch rarely get that big. We got all our fish in 14 feet of water right off the bottom.

When we got back to my house with all these big panfish we spread them out on my kitchen table and probably took twenty photos. I regret that I did not put my big perch in the freezer to mount later. How many anglers ever caught one that big in Minnesota waters? It would have made a beautiful mount but we ate it instead and it tasted great.

On November 6, 2010, Ken and I went to Boulder Lake to wet a line on open water for the last time that year. There was ice on the water at the public access but it was only a half inch thick. We had no trouble breaking the ice to get the boat in. It was a cold, cloudy and breezy day so we only stayed out three hours. Although we went to the same spot as our trip last month we got skunked. By then the water temperature was only 38. This was only the second time we had to break ice to get my boat launched. Then we put it away for the winter in my back garage. We carried my 8 hp Yamaha down to my basement again for the winter. I have never bothered to have my outboard motors winterized and it only caused a problem once. The trick is to drain out all the water before freeze up which we always did.

I missed the May walleye opener in 2011 for the first time in years since my boat was back at the Crestliner factory in Little Falls, Minnesota. When I took my rig to Gene's Marine the month before for routine motor maintenance, they noticed that the back of the transom was separating from the rest of it! Gene said he would not take my boat on the water if it was his since the back of the boat might fall off and end up on the bottom of the lake with my motors! Since my boat was still under warranty, I hired a friend named Don D. to help me get to Little Falls with it. It took the factory technicians three weeks to get it rebuilt. They took the entire transom off and disassembled it. They then installed a lot of support struts and re-assembled it. They said I would never have any more trouble with it and so far, I haven't. I was glad my Crestliner had a 20-year warranty that did not depreciate like Lund and Alumacraft boat warranties do. This is one of the main reasons I opted for the Crestliner in the first place. Furthermore, Crestliner's back then had no rivets to pop loose which causes seepage.

For Memorial weekend of 2011 we had another unusual fishing experience. Doug, Ken and I rented an ice fishing house on shore at Hunters Point resort on the east shore of Lake Mille Lacs. It had electricity but no running water, but a ceiling fan. We were close to the shower house and the resort had a café. During the first night Doug went to the shower house in the middle of the night to pee. There was a teenage boy in the bathroom sucking the boobs of a teenage girl. He watched them while urinating since they never stopped. Doug wanted to join in the fun but he figured he would just get in trouble. Those horny kids had snuck out of their parent's cabins in the night to enjoy each other and they never even slowed down during Doug's presence! Not sure how that one ended up and not sure I want to know.

Fishing and the weather were bad this weekend. On our last evening some black clouds rolled in. We were going to get off the water anyway and on Doug's last cast with his slip bobber his monofilament line went up in the air! We heard of this scary natural phenomenon but never experienced it before. We knew it was dangerous so we flew to shore just in time before the lightning started. This was caused by static electricity in the air from those black clouds and was a bit frightening.

On August 6, 2011, Ken, Doug, and I headed back to Basket Lake Camp in Ontario. This trip was postponed from June due to a state government shutdown under Governor Tim Pawlenty so we could not get across the border. We finally got across the border at Fort Francis, Ontario without difficulty again.

My new tent was weird and poor Ken spent 90 minutes trying to figure it out. Doug said he could not have got it up without Ken's help. When we finally got it done and finished supper the resort owner, Dr. Anita, paid us a visit. She told us the Weagles are coming. We did not know what a Weagle was so I asked if that is a Canadian weasel. She chortled and said that the Weagles are a large family from Wisconsin checking in late that night. She added that one of the men is low functioning and is on probation with her due to his bad temper he displayed many times in the past at her resort. Yikes! We couldn't wait to meet him!

She wasn't kidding. We crawled into our tent at ten p.m. and then they arrived in what sounded like a cavalcade! They had a huge motor home and several tents which they erected right behind us. We heard machinery running. It was an air compressor for air mattresses that sounded like a crane. Furthermore, a woman started yelling at a guy named Larry. He had a big mosquitos fogger and was chasing around individual insects with it and yelling, "I got one!" We giggled in the tent and knew which one was low functioning. We asked them to keep the noise down since we were trying to sleep. The woman apologized but the noise went on for a long time before we finally drifted off to sleep, choking on the fogger fumes, hoping we awake someday.

Our first day of fishing was great. Under perfect weather conditions we boated 40 walleyes and had a nice swim at the fish cleaning beach. WE had a huge fish fry that night with bloody Mary's. I should explain that we don't drink near as much at home as we do on a fishing excursion. Honest!

The second day we boated 44 walleyes and released most of them while fishing in the drizzle all day. We drifted a big mud Flat which was the only place we could catch any. Some were big.

On our third day on the water, we saw several tiny funnel clouds on the horizon in the afternoon. It looked like little black fingers dropping down to the trees tops over and over again from a large black wall cloud. We watched for a while and decided we better get off the water. We pulled up on shore and stood under trees smoking big cigars and sipping bourbon. To pass the time we made up a song about the Weagles and ended up singing it round robin in 3-part harmony! "the Weagles wobble but they don't fall down; They Don't fall down; they don't fall down. The Weagles wobble but they don't fall down onto the ground."

Blame it on the bourbon. We finally got out on the water again since the tornado veered off. Believe it or not we caught another 30 walleyes that day which surprised us. What a country!

The next day we had lousy weather again and had to get off the water due to lightning again. We still caught 30 fish. We finally had good weather the next day but it was windy. We boated 44 walleyes anyway.

On our last day of fishing, we had decent weather and decided to get serious about bringing home limits of eating size walleyes which was only four. Our last stop was a giant boulder at the chute where Ken caught 6 eaters in a row. Since he had naming rights, he called that spot Sin Rock. I guess the preacher was still in him even though he left the ministry by then.

By the way, the Weagles provided "entertainment" for us all week in the form of family drama. Larry kept blowing up and slamming the door to the RV. One day he slammed it so hard it fell off and then his very large wife blew up too! It was like the battling Bickersons all week! When we checked out on Saturday poor Anita confided she would never allow them to return to Basket Lake Camp. We were relieved and thanked her.

On this trip we went through two pounds of large leeches and 400 nightcrawlers. We did not use minnows at all. One of the great things about this lake was that jigs worked much better than on most Minnesota lakes which we relished. Doug caught the biggest walleye at 7 pounds. We hardly fished pike at all. Our total walleye count was 237 and 24 pike. We had no adversity or technical difficulty on this trip, fortunately. It was an uneventful ride home for a change; not even a flat tire on the trailer. Amazing!

In January of 2012 four of us guys went to upper Red Lake for some ice fishing. Red Lake is just north of Bemidji, Minnesota, home of Paul Bunyan and his Babe the Blue Ox, who stand on the shore of Lake Bemidji in statue.

Terry, Ken, Doug, and I rented a 4-bunk sleeper house from Puerta Villa resort for the first time ever. This resort had a large generator out a few miles from shore with 6 100-foot extension cord to supply electricity to six ice shelters. This was luxury since we had electric lights, a 2-burner electric range and an electric fridge. Unfortunately, we also had a heated outhouse. Yuck! At least it was not close to our dwelling which was a 7 X 16-foot wheelhouse.

Our first day was very productive, both for angling and partying. We caught many walleyes and even had a triple which is rare for ice fishing. I pulled in the biggest walleye on my rattle reel, a 22.5 incher. Terry cleaned fish outside on the fish cleaning table provided by the resort. For some reason he cleaned those fish without a shirt on. Macho, I guess.

The next day fishing slowed down so I laid on my bunk to rest. I still had my line down the hole next to my bunk. It was a short rod and reel with a big minnow. Half asleep I heard a weird noise. My rod just flew down the hole! I started cussing but only about three minutes later Ken had a major bite. After about five minutes he pulled in a 6-pound pike with his hook and mine in its toothy mouth, both lip hooked. Up the hole popped my rod and reel, to my delight!

We pulled in a few more walleyes but decided to have steaks for supper so we could take home our limits of fillets which was 2four fish. Steak in an ice fishing shack tastes even better. The morning we departed we caught no more fish but we were happy and had no adversity on this trip. It was a happy drive back to Cloquet.

On June 2, 2012 Ken and I went to Mille lacs and fished the Blue Jug structure. We found the weed bed in 23 feet of water. We trolled it for a while and I boated a 4 pounder, a 5 pounder and a 6 pounder. The latter made a run straight out from the boat and then turned and charged the boat. I raised up my arms and reeled as fast as I could. As soon as we got it in the net the hook fell out of the critters mouth. Ken said that fish had gray eyes and a grayish tinge. We speculated it was probably a very old male and we released it alive. I got a couple of eaters on the rocks in Agate Bay that evening but poor Ken got skunked. He had a six pounder on the surface but it got unhooked before he netted it.

At the end of September of 2012 Roger and Mike drove up from St. Cloud to help me celebrate my birthday with some fishing. Mike's too. We drove up to Trout Lake in Coleraine, Minnesota since we had a hot tip. The water was gin clear and it was a bright, sunny day so we only caught one walleye. Roger boated a 23 incher which we released since it was in the slot. It was a hot day and we had fun skinny dipping and drinking beer in the boat. We left the water at 8:30 with five giant sunfish. We drove back to my house in Cloquet for late night pizza from Sammy's. We stayed up late drinking and singing along to Beatles music which Mike requested. We must have sung along to "Rocky Raccoon" at least ten times!

The next day we made the mistake of fishing Wild Rice Lake by Duluth for the first time ever. The deepest water we could find was 8 feet and there were rock hazards everywhere. We hardly caught a thing and we clipped off one of the tines on my big motors' prop. We vowed never to return to that little lake. The highlight was listening to the Vikings victory on my radio in the boat. It was a grand birthday and I thanked them for visiting me.

Due to ice on the lakes in northern Minnesota, there was no open water fishing for the opener in 2013. This was very unusual and we were not happy about it since this event is a long-standing tradition. It is so fun to "make the scene." It is about excitement and adventure just like this book.

In early July of 2013 Ken and I embarked on new territory. We trailered my rig to Devils Lake North Dakota. We heard stories about great walleye and jumbo perch fishing and wanted to sample it. It was a very long drive of 350 miles. We camped at Gramm Island State Park which is on a island connected by a narrow road that was obviously built just to get to that spot. We found a secluded campsite and pitched our tent.

When we talked to others in the park, they were all surprised that we brought a boat. They said most nice walleyes in Devils Lake were caught from shore in May and June. We did not know this and figured the fish have to eat all summer, not just in May and June.

That prairie body of water is so big that any wind causes big problems. The wind never stopped the whole time we were there. Fishing was lousy but one day we boated to a giant tree that was half above the surface. I actually tied the boat to a tree branch so we could do some vertical jigging. I boated an 8-pound pike but no walleyes.

Many buildings and trees are under water in this weird lake since the water level keeps rising each year. There are three inlets flowing into Devils Lake and only one outlet so the water level just keeps rising. There are actually barns under water!

On the third day of restricted fishing due to winds Ken said he was depressed. I replied that it's not possible to get depressed on a fishing trip. After a pause he said he invited his son's family to visit him from Omaha this same week. When I asked why he scheduled a visit when he was on a fishing trip, he said he got his weeks mixed up and did not realize it until a couple of days before we were to depart for North Dakota. I then asked him if he had a calendar. He replied that he did but he never looked at it since he thought he could remember his schedule. He said he wanted to go home.

I had a sinking feeling and there was a long silence as I needed to think about ending our trip at midpoint. I told him the winds would probably die out tomorrow so we could move around more and probably catch more fish. This did not fly and after a while I reluctantly agreed to go home early. I deduced that if I said no, he would just make the rest of our trip miserable. We pulled up the boat and packed up our camp. After a long, unhappy and quiet ride we finally got to my house after midnight. Ken was grumpy and irritable which I had never seen in him before. I could not understand why he was acting this way in view of the fact that he got his way. At any rate, he decided he was too tired to drive the additional 100 miles to his home in North branch, Minnesota. He spent the night at my house. I assumed he would be off early the next morning since he was eager to be with his family. Instead, he helped me run some errands and left late that afternoon.

I came home with one limit of small walleyes all of which were caught at dusk on slip bobbers. We decided we would never go back to Devils Lake since it is a very weird lake and certainly not worth the long drive. At least North Dakota allows an angler to keep more fish than Minnesota; ten.

In late August of 2013 roger and Mike drove up to Cloquet from St. cloud to fish Island Lake again which they loved. Mid-afternoon we finally hit the fishing bonanza. The smallmouth bass went on a rampage. Roger caught a 21 incher and I boated a 17.5 incher as well as several three pounders. Mike had the biggest one on. This smallmouth did cartwheels on the surface and then barreled perpendicular out from the side of the boat. It turned and made a mad dash for the boat. Mike reeled as fast as he could but there was still slack in the line so he lost that one. They both said it looked like a six pounder: certainly, the biggest of the day.

About that time the rear battery went dead so we hooked my jumper cables connecting both marine batteries and it worked! We ran all devices off the rear battery and the power anchor off the front one. I never dreamed of such an ingenious maneuver but roger had this creative notion so kudos to him.

When we finally left Island Lake, we had 29 fish in the live well: 10 sunfish, 9 small walleyes and 10 big perch. We had a great day on the water and they said they wanted to return to that large lake by Duluth.

In June of 2014 Mike, roger and I fished Fish Lake by Duluth. It was a beautiful and warm sunny day. We skinny dipped and caught lots of good sized panfish. We had a fish fry that night but Roger would not cook many of them since he wanted to take them all home for himself. He was always greedy as well as gregarious. He was also very tight fisted even though he is a multi-millionaire who lives in a mansion that has an elevator. We often teased him about this discrepancy. He got worse as the years rolled by. Mike and I have always known he and I are roger's only non-millionaire friends. Should we consider ourselves lucky? Roger is also the best fisherman I have ever known. The fish just seem to follow him around. Of course, it really enhances his productivity on the water that he always fishes with at least three lines and never gets busted for it. I will always be grateful to him for helping me get through my divorce in 1995.

In February of 2015 Terry, Ken and I drove to Twin River Resort on the Minnesota side of Lake of the Woods. Our 3-bedroom cabin on shore was just 8 miles past Baudette, Minnesota. We were very happy we each had our own room since we all snore like cavemen. We checked in on a Friday night which was bitterly cold. The next morning my van would not start. We used the resorts jump pack but to no avail. We had no alternative but to call a tow truck. Fortunately, I have Triple A or the truck would not have driven all the way up from Blackduck, MN which was the closest towing company.

When he finally arrived, he could not get it started either but by crawling under my van was able to determine that it was my starter that was bad. We got in his truck and rode to Blackduck with him, van in tow. He was also a mechanic with his own garage, so he ordered the part from nearby Bemidji, and it was at his shop by the time we got there.

He dropped us off at a local café for our second breakfast of the morning to kill time while he did the repair job. The cute little waitress, who had a funny name, kept flirting with me. She even told me her apartment was just a block away and she was about to take her lunch hour. Apparently, she wanted a quickie with me. Since I did not know her at all I was not interested in passion with her. To get rid of her I pulled out my white cane and told her I am blind. She disappeared and never came back just like they always do when they learn I am blind.

After spending $308. On repairs we got back to our cabin at 2:30. Since we knew it would be dark at 4:30 we figured it made no sense to make the hour long 21 mile drive out to our rental house so we took naps and then drank vodka with our supper and happy hour.

The next morning the van started and we finally got to fish. We were grateful the ice houses were numbered. We actually drove over an island which is where the plowed road took us. Fishing was mediocre that day and it did not help that I forgot my bucket that had my rods and tackle box. Ken had an extra rod for me. It wasn't long after that I dropped my folding white cane down my ice hole! Yikes! We laughed and I stated that it's probably the only white cane ever dropped on the bottom of that inland sea. Such a claim to fame!

We caught nine eater walleyes that day. I pulled in the biggest at 21 inches. When Terry was taking the hook out the fish jerked and drove the hook into his hand. After a lot of cussing and some bloodshed we got him bandaged up. I got all mine on a Swedish pimple with a minnow head.

Ken had the idea that if we put our walleyes in my van, they would not freeze that afternoon even though the temp was around zero. When we got to shore at dark, they were nearly frozen solid. We thawed them in the heated fish cleaning house for two hours while we had another very happy hour before a delicious fish fry.

We went back out the next morning for a half day of fishing but only caught three more eaters which buoyed us for the long ride back to Cloquet. Although the angling was nothing to write home about, we had fun anyway as well as lots of male bonding. Another good trip in the books.

I retired in June of 2015 and then moved to Rochester, Minnesota to be near my elderly mother who lived in assisted living. She needed my help and companionship. It was not an easy decision since Olmsted County is one of only four counties in Minnesota that has no natural lakes. It has a few little ponds and a reservoir which is basically a sewer full of rough fish. I knew I would have to experiment with fishing the nearby Mississippi river. Yuck!

I also had to leave behind several friends in Duluth, but I needed to put my sweet mother first. Besides, I have caught tens of thousands of fish in my life and I knew we would still be going to Canada every summer. These thoughts consoled me.

In September of 2015 Mike and roger came to visit me for some birthday fishing. We reluctantly drove to the Mississippi river by Wabasha, Minnesota. It was a bizarre experience on the water. There was a trawler dredging out the main channel. We had never seen this before and it was very noisy. We figured the noise would spook the fish but a while later Mike hooked something big just 80 feet from that trawler. He thought it was a snagged bottom since we were fishing in just eight feet of water, but it started moving and jerking.

Mike was using an ultralight with six-pound test mono, so he had to be gentle with the big brute. After about 15 minutes it finally came up. It was a huge catfish, the biggest fish of his life! Roger netted it but had trouble lifting it into the boat since he is a little guy. We high fived and marveled at its size. Each of us held it up and took photos on their smart phones. It weighed out at nearly 30 pounds! Of course, he released it. This was the biggest fish ever in my boat. We never boated a game fish that day but it was still a good birthday for me and I was grateful they drove down from St. Cloud to visit me.

On April Fool's Day of 2016 Ken and I drove my boat and van to Bismark, North Dakota to fish the Missouri River with his brother-in-law, Ryan. Upon arrival at his house, we discovered he had no food in his fridge, so we ate out every meal except for a fish fry one night. Ryan was a poor host and grumpy all weekend. Ken warned me beforehand that Ryan is always that way. We decided to try it anyway since we love new adventures.

We got there Friday night after a 500-mile cruise from Rochester to Bismark. We set up our cots in his barren spare bedroom of his apartment. After a couple of nightcaps, we retired. It was a rough night. Ken snored like a freight train and twice I woke him up because he sounded like he was choking in his sleep. I slept three hours that night so was in no shape to spend the next day on the water so They went out without me. To top it off the high temp for the day was to be 34 degrees F with a windchill of 22! I knew I would be miserable in the boat, exhausted and shivering. Staying alone in his apartment was very boring but I rested all day. They stayed on the water all day and came in with six small walleyes which we ate. That second night Ken slept on the couch in the living room, for my benefit. I was grateful and thanked him.

We fished 20 miles south of Bismark the second day. We caught nine walleyes but no big ones. We got them on jigs and minnows in 10 feet of water. I caught the first shad of my life. It was a 5 pounder with a silverish color and a small mouth. It put up a good fight. We also caught two small sturgeon, the first ever in my boat. They were weird and prehistoric looking. We released them and the shad, too.

That day we were fishing just a few miles from the grave of Lakota Chief Sitting Bull. I wanted to visit that site for sentimental reasons but the guys were not interested.

The third day was very windy so we were confined to a small bay. However, the crappie fishing was great with bobbers. We boated 15 crappies, all in the 1-to-2-pound range which is big for Midwest crappies. Ryan had a bigger one on the surface but it got away just as Ken was lunging for it with the landing net. They said it was a pounder. All the crappies were the black strain which seem to get a little larger than the white ones. We were bereft of walleyes that day.

We left for home on Monday. Ken and I listened to loud classical music all the way home. He cranked up the rear speakers in my van which made it sound like a small concert hall on wheels. Five times on the way home we had the same thought at the same time and once we even spoke out loud the exact same sentence at the same time! We were definitely on the same wavelength but it was a bit eerie. Finally, we decided that 500 miles was too far to go for a few eaters, so we never went back. However, we were glad we did this trip as it was another adventure for the books and a new one at that.

On May 20, 2016 Ken and I drove to Robards Lake by Faribault. Fishing was dead even with perfect weather. The barometer was sky high and the full moon did not help. At 2 pm we pulled up the boat and went to French lake, just a mile away. We could not get the boat off the trailer. We then discovered we left the boat straps on! We pulled forward and removed the straps. The boat rolled off the trailer easily. Just before we boated away from the dock, we realized we forgot to put the drain plug back in and were taking on water! I had just had a new drain plug system installed so by turning the knob on the transom we closed the drain. We bilged out quite a bit of water which took a while. Although we got skunked on French too, we laughed at ourselves all afternoon because of our silly mistakes. We agreed we are both a couple of born losers! LOL When we finally came off the lake, we saw that we never did put the padlock on the trailer tongue that day. Luckily, no one drove off with our trailer. It was a Laurel and Hardy kind of day.

On Memorial Day of 2016 Mike and roger drove down from St. Cloud again to fish with me. We drove to Robards Lake. There was a line of boats waiting to launch. Roger used that time to scout the guys coming off the lake. One guy had limits of walleyes and roger asked where he got them. We finally launched and drove to that spot. We fished in 10 to 12 feet of water near some weeds, less than a mile from the public access. Using panfish jigs and baby leeches we caught 35 walleyes but none were huge. We kept our three-man limit of 18. Mike had the biggest at 17.5 inches and mine was close behind. All of Roger's fish were small but he insisted on keeping his limit of them anyway, as usual.

When we got back to my house in Rochester, they cleaned our catch with their electric fillet knife which was quick and easy. We had a major fish fry with the original Shore Lunch batter and wild rice from northern Minnesota lakes. It was superb!

On July 9 of 2016, Ken and I tried Robards Lake once again. As usual it was a bust with Ken. Sometimes I wondered if he and I are jinxes together. Perfect weather did not help possibly due to high barometer. I got the only gamefish of the day; a sunfish. Ken caught several sheephead, otherwise known as freshwater drum. He kept three and I said they are so gross he will have to clean them in my garage instead of my kitchen table. When he filleted them out, they had nice white fillets just like walleyes and he took them home. A couple of days later he called with a culinary report. He said the sheephead fillets tasted fine but the texture was so awful he spit it out and threw them all away. His lovely wife would not eat them either. He never tried that again. Somehow, I refrained from saying "I told you so."

On July 25 of 2016, Doug, Tyler and I pitched my tent at Stoney Point Chippewa campground on the south shore of Leech Lake. It was a federal campsite without any staff at all. Very weird. At least it was not crowded. As usual, we had trouble erecting my tent and Doug and Ty got a little heated. We finally got camp set up and hit the water around 4 pm.

I missed a nice jerk on my lure because the anti-reverse lever on my reel was off so I could not set the hook. A rookie mistake. Doug boated two eater walleyes but we saw none caught by anyone else. There were few boats on the water. The next day fishing actually got worse. We did not catch a single walleye; just a 3-pound pike which we released. We tried leeches, crawlers, jigs, spinners and harnesses as well as slip bobbers.

Tyler, now age 24, got drunk the night before and had a rough stomach in the boat. He threw up over the side of my boat. His "chumming" did not help the angling. However, the loons serenaded us all day which was beautiful.

That night we had a torrential downpour all night. We were shocked my tent did not leak. It wasn't letting up so finally Doug got up at 9 a.m. and cooked bacon and eggs in the rain in the back of my van. He actually served Ty and I breakfast in bed which made us feel a little like royalty.

We knew walleyes would not bite after the all-night thunderstorm, so we drove into Walker to Shriver's Baits to ask about a good sunfish lake in the area. Apparently, the guy had pity on the guy with the white cane and directed us to May/Long lake where his own house sat. It was hard to find and difficult to get into but we made it. Just as we were getting the boat ready to launch two cute young girls dressed in bikinis and wearing little short robes walked across the access with a 6 pack of wine coolers. They walked over to a small nearby point where they had innertubes waiting. They tossed their little robes onto the rocks and paddled out onto the water, beverages in hand. When we got on the water Tyler watched them for a while. When the girls got too far away, he got out my trusty binoculars to scope them out. He reported that the girls were now topless and applying sunscreen lotion to their boobs. Tyler missed a few fish that afternoon.

We only caught Four nice sunnies on Long Lake so we went through the small, shallow channel into May Lake. As soon as we dropped the anchor and we struck gold. We pounded a lot of bluegills and big pumpkinseeds. I dropped my line without a bobber. When it hit the bottom in 8 feet of water, I reeled up one foot of line and hooked one after another. The guys were getting them on slip bobbers. A few of them were pounders. We came off the water around 8 with 30 in the live well. We did not want Doug to fry fish in the dark so we had supper at Hardees in Walker.

The next morning, we started the day with a nice fish fry and lots of coffee brewed in the great outdoors in my stove top percolator. We fished Leech Lake all that day. It was boring since we caught nothing. We had a nice campfire that night and a couple of nightcaps.

The next morning, we packed up since we only had the campsite until that day. However, we went back to May Lake to catch a dozen nice sunfish. We had supper at Dairy Queen and got back to Doug's at dark.

On September 12, 2016, Doug, Tyler, and I reunited for more angling. This time we slept at Doug's house in Andover every night. Tyler was nice enough to give me his bed and he took the couch.

The first day we fished Chisago Lake which is about 30 miles north of the metro. It was a great day of pan-fishing and we came off the water with 38 sunfish and one crappie. We had a good breakfast fish fry the next day before going to West Rush Lake. It was poor fishing, so we boated into East Rush Lake and did much better. The crappies were biting on everything and we came off the lake with 29, just one short of 3 limits.

The next day Tyler stayed home while Doug and I went to Green Lake. We had perfect weather and lots of sunfish and crappie but the power anchor was troublesome all week.

When we pulled the boat out of the water the winch strap, which was the original, broke off. Fortunately, we had the boat all the way up on the trailer and were able to hook up the safety chain. Otherwise, I don't know how we could push the heavy boat the rest of the way onto the sloped trailer.

The next morning over coffee Doug and I agreed we should not use the boat again without a new winch strap. We took the rig to Rapids Marine in Ham Lake, Minnesota and they were not busy. In just three hours' time, they replaced the winch strap and installed a new power anchor. The only power anchor unit left was the display model which I bought at a $90. Discount. The total cost was $360. Which I did not mind. I already knew at that point that boats are money pits but well worth it.

In October of 2016, Mike and Roger drove down from St. Cloud again to fish Lake Robards near Faribault. We slammed the fish at our first spot in 13 feet of water in front of a mansion. We only fished three hours before we ran out of crappie minnows. We came home with nine eater walleyes and 30 jumbo perch. Mike nailed the biggest walleye at just under 18 inches. We had perfect weather and a lot of fun. Of course, that night we had the obligatory fish fry with roger's home-made batter, which he claimed was the best in the world. It was indeed delicious.

Just a week later Ken and I finished off the year of open water fishing on Robards Lake. As usual, fishing was slow. Suddenly, I got a snag. I asked Ken to move the boat forward so I could pull it out from the other direction. Right then, my rod started jerking. It was a fish! I was using an ultralight for the panfish so the brute had its way with me. I finally got it close enough for Ken to net it. It was a ten-pound pike I had lip hooked perfectly somehow. I told Ken if he would clean it for me, I would give him half the meat. He agreed and I tossed it in the live well which was filling up. When it was full of water the fish slammed against the underside of the lid and the lid popped up a couple of inches! We had never seen this before or since. When I opened the lid to check on it the pike made a loud huffing noise! I never heard this noise from a fish before either and did not know pike could huff. I actually felt a little guilty about killing that critter but we wanted something to eat and Ken's wife was always thrilled when he brought home his catch for her. That fish crapped in my boat. So ends another great year of sportfishing with loved ones!

CHAPTER TEN: THE FINAL YEARS

In June of 2017 Doug, Tyler and I drove to Sauk Lake to pitch our tent at Saukinac Camp. We were the only campers so had lots of room. This site was like an aviary. There were so many beautiful birds around us we had few mosquitos and the birdsongs were pretty. That evening Ty boated a 24-inch walleye which we kept to eat for breakfast the next morning since he was allowed to keep one bigger fish.

Unfortunately, that night was a true nightmare. Shortly after we got to sleep, we were awakened by two drunk guys yelling. When we looked out the tent screen window Doug saw them in a boat close to our camp. They had bows and were shining for carp which they were shooting. They yelled for two hours so it was impossible to sleep. We finally got back to sleep at first light except for Doug. When we got up that morning we were fried and poor Doug reported he got only one hour of sleep. It was not a good way to start our adventure. We had never heard of shooting carp on Sauk Lake but we knew it was connected to Sauk River which joins with the Mississippi River downstream.

That day we were in no shaped to fish well and Doug would not try hardly anything but bobber fishing. All we got were a few perch. When we came in that night the resort owner said the DNR had stocked Sauk Lake with so many walleyes there weren't many panfish left. He directed us to Fairy Lake on the other side of Sauk Center so we went there the next day.

Fairy lake was a beautiful little lake with clear water and a nice, sandy beach. We probably caught 200 sunfish but most of them were the size of large potato chips. We only kept 12 bigger ones. By this time the boys were frustrated. To make matters worse Tyler, who was not very coordinated, stepped on his favorite Fenwick ultralight rod and broke it right in the boat. He threw a fit and stomped his feet, yelling out his frustration. By now the mood was spoiled despite perfect weather.

Furthermore, we had weird electrical problems in my boat that made no sense at all. The live well pump and bilge pump stopped working and the locator kept shutting off. Then the tilt and trim on my big motor malfunctioned so the motor would not stop going up and down so I had to unhook a cable from the battery terminal. Tyler said he is a jinx and I silently wondered if he was right. We knew it was time to depart so we picked up a 12 pack of beer and drove back to camp with the nectar of the gods.

We made pork chops on the Coleman stove with veggies and beer for supper. We had a very nice talk around the campfire that night which helped. To cap off our day the rain started at dusk so we dragged the cooler into my tent for a tent party which was fun. We had everything we needed including a pee jug, a battery lantern and radio as well as a multitude of Beverages and much laughter. It poured for a long time but my new tent did not leak for once and we managed to finish off the disappointing day on a positive note.

However, it rained all night and the forecast was for rain all day so we packed up the wet tent and went home the next morning.

We dropped off Tyler at their home in Ramsey before Doug drove me home to Rochester. About 20 miles north of Rochester we had yet another flat tire on the trailer, passengers' side as usual.

It was ten p.m. and dark but I had a lantern. It turned out we had stopped in front of the home of a good Samaritan. He came out with a big spotlight to help out with the tire change. Shortly thereafter, a big truck pulled up behind my boat. He was headed north and decided to turn around to assist us. He said he only stopped because we were fishermen. We got the spare tire on but it was low, but the house guy had an air compressor, so we pumped it up. All the while, we were having fun joking around and the truck guy said he was in no hurry to get home to his wife anyway. We all chortled. We finally made it to my house and crashed.

In mid-July of that year Mike and roger came down from St. cloud again to fish the Faribault lakes which they loved. On the first day we were on Robards lake and got totally skunked. The water was 84 degrees. The next day we hit Shields Lake nearby and boated about 100 sunfish. We kept 60 which was the limit for three guys. The water temp was 77 and mini-mites were deadly even without bait. None were a pound but we had a great fish fry that night. I introduced them to Moscow mules which they loved!

At the end of September of 2017 Ken drove down from St. Paul to help me celebrate my birthday with some crappie fishing on Cedar Lake by Faribault. It was very windy so we dropped the anchor between two islands for shelter. This worked well and we caught lots of crappies and kept some. I also caught a 5-pound pike on my ultralight which was fun. The crappies were aggressive until the rain started at 3 o'clock. Since it was so windy, we could not get the boat on the trailer straight and for the first time in years we had to back it into the water to start over.

In June of 2018, Doug, Tyler, and I went back to shields Lake by Faribault where Doug practically grew up fishing with his dad. We found a very small bay that Doug recalled from his childhood. We dropped the anchor in three feet of water. There were hundreds of red wing blackbirds nesting in that wooded cove. They serenaded us all afternoon with their beautiful birdsong and the bay was ringed with blossoming lily pads. It was idyllic.

I hooked a big pike that looked to be a ten pounder. It bit off my mini jig on the surface so we missed it. However, we boated lots of sunfish and came home with 25. It was another special day on the water and another great fish fry that night in my kitchen. Somehow Doug stumbled out of my boat in my garage and gouged his leg and bruised his heel. Not sure how this happened since he can see and has very long legs. We chalked it up to the four beers he had while cleaning fish as well as cooking and eating them; the wuss.

On July 23, 2018, Doug, Tyler and I, ever the three stooges, checked into Sugar point Resort on Leech Lake. We pitched my tent near an octagonal picnic table and hit the water right after burgers. We fished until dark in Portage Bay and only boated one eater walleye.

The next day was a cold front with a massive mayfly hatch. The water was covered with billions of them. We only caught two fish all day, both pike, which we kept to eat, just in case we had poor walleye fishing in the next couple of days. The next day was a Monday and there was a big professional walleye tournament on the lake. There were many large, expensive boats on the water, all decked out with sponsors decals. The hatch was still in full force. We caught no fish all day and only saw one netted by other boats all day. At supper Doug said this was the first time in his life he never got a bite all day.

We tried all our spots that usually worked; Ginza rock, Bear Island submarine island and Portage Bay but to no avail. The next day there was no bug hatch and we nailed five walleyes between 23 and 26 inches. I caught a five pounder on a Phelps floater and leech which was my only walleye of the week.

That morning I woke up with a lot of pain in my neck for the first time ever which persisted for days. With lots of ibuprofen and some afternoon whiskey I got through the week. To top things off, that night around the campfire, my lawn chair collapsed and I went down. Somehow, I did not get hurt and did not even spill my drink. We had a good laugh and Tyler threw the chair in the dumpster.

On our last day of angling, we had to get off the lake twice for lightning and we suffered through yet another mayfly hatch. We decided to throw in the towel and packed up my tent in the rain which really sucked. One of the few highlights was having supper at the Big Fish supper club in Bena, Minnesota which had a fantastic chicken special. That club has a giant walleye statue in front so we had to get photos of ourselves hamming it up next to it. On the way home Doug and I decided to give up on Leech Lake due to little fishing success over a number of trips. Leech is a great lake for insects but not for fishing. Furthermore, any wind at all on this big water greatly restricts our movement; just too hard.

In mid-August of 2018 Ken and I wanted to fish the Faribault lakes one Saturday, but John at John's Baits in Faribault said all the area lakes but Cannon were slimed over with green algae. Dog days. Therefore, we reluctantly went to fish the Mississippi out of Kellogg, Minnesota. We found a ramshackle bait shop in town that looked like the old Hany Place in Green Acres. Next to its front Door stood a snow shovel with a tree branch for a handle. Pa Kettle would have been proud. We had a feeling we were about to have an unusual experience and we were right.

When we got inside the old guy working there looked like he had to be at least a hundred years old. He had his scanner volume so loud we could not believe it. Furthermore, his TV was also blasting so we had a hard time communicating. We bought our bait and asked him where to fish and he snarled, "how the hell should I know? No one ever tells me anything!" It was clear to us why this was true. Grumpy old man. He sent us to a nearby public access that was closed so we went two miles further downstream to a nice access that was actually open.

I caught a small walleye and Ken boated a big sheephead. Then I hooked something huge. I fought it for a long time and at one point most of the line in my spinning reel was out. I finally got it under the boat when it got unhooked. We never did see it but we figured it was a big catfish.

It was 89 degrees that afternoon and by this time we needed a break. Ken spotted an island about a mile downstream that had a big tree hanging out over the water. Shade! We took off as best we could with our damaged prop from running aground. We dropped anchor under that big branch. We had heard many times that fish congregate under tree branches. Unfortunately, no one told those river fish they were supposed to be there. We got no fish or even a bite although we charted some.

Just before we left Ken said, "a snake dropped into the boat!" At first, I thought he was kidding since I had never heard of a snake falling into a boat. As he described the 3-foot garter snake I became convinced. I said, "Ken, I really don't feel like having a snake in my boat right now so how about if you flip that baby into the river?" He did so without getting bit. When we parked under that branch, we certainly did not know there was a snake waiting for us.

We decided this meant we are supposed to call it quits for today and headed for the landing since we were nearly snake bit. When we were trailered up, we took off for Slippery's Cafe in Wabasha, featured in that famous movie "Grumpy Old Men which was filmed in Wabasha and starred Walter Mathau, Jack Lemon and the lovely Ann Margaret.

When we got to Slippery's the waitress said the restaurant was full so we had to eat at the bar, which we didn't mind too terribly much! Somehow, I ended up next to a woman that had the most Martian-like voice I had ever heard! She talked just like an alien robot and I began to wonder what world she is from. When I finally asked her about her voice she laughed and said everyone thinks she is from outer space! Good thing she was drunk. Right about that time her food arrived from the kitchen: deep fried alligator! Now I was pretty much convinced she was some sort of reptilian being! She actually offered me a piece of the gator. I decided to risk it. yuck! My Slippery's Burger was fantastic and the ice-cold beer wasn't too shabby either.

As we drove home Ken and I could not decide if we were just in Green Acres, Grumpy Old Men or a Martian sitcom! After much chuckling debate we concluded it was all three. By the way, that was the only time I ever had a snake in the boat or ate with a Martian, but hopefully not the last! All in a day's fishing, right?

In the fall of 2018, Mike and Roger drove down from St. Cloud once again to fish with me. We trailered the glory van and CLOUD 9, my boat, to Cedar Lake by Faribault. We hit the crappie jackpot. In 20 to 27 feet of water by and island we boated about 80 fish. The locator was lit up all morning and fish alarm was going off nearly all the time. We kept 45 which was the limit for three guys. When I was in the boat my friend Karla called and sang happy birthday to me. We left the lake at 2 pm since we had our limit and ran out of crappie minnows. When we got back to my townhouse, we cleaned the fish and the guys departed for home without our usual fish fry. We each had a nice bag of fillets. It was a pretty low-key day compared to our recent outing on the Mississippi River.

In January of 2019, Ken and I drove to Red Lake where we had a sleeper house reserved for two nights with Puerta Villa resorts. Our 2-bunk house had electricity which was great. I was on antibiotics for the two days before we left and not fully recovered. That first morning I woke up shivering and could not stop. We had to leave and Ken did most of the packing up. Our shelter was too chilly this time. We could not get off the lake due to a white out so we called the resort to escort us off the lake which they did. I apologized to Ken for ruining our trip but we only caught one walleye anyway. I should not have gone in the first place, but I just couldn't resist. It was a long, slow ride home with poor visibility.

Late in June of 2019, Doug, Tyler and I went to Cutfoot Sioux Lake by Deer River, Minnesota We rented a campsite at Mosomo Point Campground which is a very primitive federal site. There was no shower house or fish cleaning house but only an outhouse and an old fashion pump for water. We were grateful they were not situated close to each other!

We waited in the van for an hour for the rain to stop. We finally got the tent up and cots installed in time for an early supper. We hit the water for the evening bite with great anticipation. We only caught two walleyes to keep; the others were a bit too large. That night Tyler, ever the pyro, took two hours to get a campfire started since everything was wet.

The next day started with bacon and eggs on the Coleman stove and a big pot of strong coffee. The weather was good and we boated nice walleyes. I got four while backtrolling with a beaver flicker and leech in 20 feet of water. The beaver flicker is a small hook with a tiny willow leaf blade above it and hard to find but usually deadly. Doug was convinced so switched to that same lure and did well ending up with a skinny 26 incher. Unfortunately, we had showers in the afternoon and the fishing slowed. We had steak in the drizzle for supper on Doug's grill which was delicious even in the showers.

The next day was perfect weather all day. Seventy-eight degrees and a little ripple on the water. We fished most of the day in Big Winnie Lake which joins Cutfoot Sioux. We drifted the mud flats and caught them in 30 feet of water but nothing huge. There were few boats on the lake and we were shocked we got no snags all week which was unheard of! After a tequila happy hour and a supper of giant cheeseburgers we hit Williams Narrows, which connects the two lakes. We bobber fished and I got two right under the boat with nightcrawlers, one a 21 incher. We had a great campfire party that night with tons of mosquitos.

The next morning fishing was slow. The weather forecast for the afternoon was for a hailstorm so we packed up and went home. The lake water was cold, not even 70 degrees, so we could not bathe in the lake. One afternoon I took a sponge bath in the boat since I could not stand my odor any longer. Doug and Tyler went stinky all week. We decided to never go back to that campground. We did not need to rough it that much but the price was right and it was very secluded; total wilderness with lots of loons and pelicans but few boats. Just the way we like it. I came home with two walleyes that were at the maximum allowable length. Poor Tyler only boated two walleyes all week.

I bought the boys baby back ribs at Q Fanatics when we got home.

Parenthetically, when we were pulling my boat out of the water a bird landed on top of my outboard motor right in front of me to watch us. A lady game warden was there and said it was her pet, Jack. Then Jack landed on the window ledge of my van! When she called it the bird landed on her finger!

For this adventure I decided to break the promise I made to myself to never bring tequila again due to that English river debacle noted above. Both Doug and Tyler liked tequila, especially the latter. However, they had exotic tastes for this stuff so I knew if I brought high grade tequila, I would not get much of it. Therefore, I bought a bottle of low-grade stuff and some high grade and swapped the contents of each bottle. Sure enough, they would not touch the Montezuma tequila all week and actually made fun of me for swilling such rotgut. On our last night around the campfire, I confessed to them of my practical joke regarding the switcheroo. They laughed a lot and swore at me even more. Then they polished off the 1800 brand with gusto and merriment!

That fall of 2019 I took the Rochester Shuttle to the Mall of America where Ken picked me up. We grabbed some burgers on the way to Glenwood, Minnesota where we stayed two nights at his in-law's house near Lake Minnewashka. It was a big place so we each had our own bedrooms. The next morning, we ate an early and hearty breakfast at Travelers Inn in downtown Alexandria. Then we met Mike, roger, his brother Bill and nephew John and headed for Fish Lake. It was a crappie jackpot!

It only took about three hours to get our six limits of keeper crappies. Green or chartreuse jibs worked best with crappie minnows.

It was a beautiful fall day of 60 degrees and sunshine so we pulled up and took both Bills and rogers boats to Lake Irene for some sunfish. The bluegills weren't really biting so after getting just 15 keepers we went to Bills garage for fish cleaning and beer. All five of those hombres cleaned all 80 fish in about two hours. We couldn't have a fish fry though since Bill promised his wife to attend a concert that night. John, Roger, and Mike drove back to St. Cloud while Ken and I had supper at the Pike & Pint restaurant in Alexandria. We had great rib eye steaks. That night we had cognac nightcaps and drove home the next morning. I came home with 30 panfish. Ken was nice enough to drive me to Rochester so I would not have to take the shuttle again.

In early May of 2020, Doug and I fished Rush Lake just north of the metro. It was a perfect spring day. We found a small lagoon and spent the entire afternoon in one spot. There were no other boats around. It was a true panfish jamboree. Doug has always had a nose for finding sunfish and we probably boated 150 of them that sunny afternoon. Our slip bobbers usually went down right away. I could not see mine but Doug was always very good about telling me when it shot down so I did not miss too many. The sunnies went nuts on mini-mites and waxworms in 3 feet of cool water. We kept 48 when the legal limit was 30 each. We wondered why no one came to fish that bay but we loved it. It was another idyllic day.

For the walleye opener of 2020 we fished Chisago Lake north of
the metro area of the Twin Cities. Walleye fishing was lousy in
the cold front, so we only kept two eaters and about 29 panfish.
There were a lot of boats around as usual on opening day in
Minnesota, but we saw few landing nets in action.

By late afternoon the wind was really picking up and we had
enough fish so we headed for the dock. There was a line of
boats waiting and by the time it was our turn there were major
whitecaps. It was one of those floating docks that was tethered
to the bottom and had some give to it. As I crawled onto the
shaky dock a giant wave slammed against the starboard side of
my boat which, in turn, jerked the boat against the dock. This
jolted the dock sideways and I went over sideways just as I was
in the process of standing. I did not fall off the dock but felt a
crunch in my left leg just above the ankle. I went down,
grabbing my leg. I laid there for a while until Doug got the van
on the ramp. Ken held me up since I could not walk unaided. He
said, "its not broken or you couldn't walk on it." When he got
me into the van, I took five ibuprofen. When we finally got to
Doug's he cleaned and cooked our catch and was my bartender.
With lots of ibuprofen and liquid pain medicine in the form of
honey bourbon I got through the night.

The next morning my toes on that left foot were black so I
figured I had a bad sprain. Doug drove me and the boat to
Rochester. I called my sister the next day since she is a nurse.
She also said it couldn't be broken or I could not walk on it.
After resting for five days my leg was no better so I called for a
doctor appointment. The soonest I could get in was another five
days away. The x-rays confirmed I had a fractured fibula which
is the smaller bone in our calf. She told me to wear a big clunky

boot which her nurse gave me. The nurse did not know how to operate the inflating mechanism and neither did I. A friend had to show me a few days later. For several weeks I lurched around the house like Frankenstein's monster! It never did mend so after walking around on a broken leg for seven months I got it surgically repaired by an orthopedic surgeon that December.

The doctor said he has never heard of anyone walking around with a broken leg for seven months. I spent Christmas in bed but luckily my sister was here and did a great job of caring for me since I was bedridden. It's a luxury to have a nurse in the family.

Believe it or not, all of my three dock accidents noted in this book occurred while I was totally sober! Honest. Furthermore, you should know that we drink a lot less at home than on our trips. We do this to celebrate!

Not to be slowed down from my fishing therapy, two weeks after I broke my leg, I was back in my boat on German Lake with Doug and ross near St. Peter, Minnesota. Ross greeted me, "howdy hop-a-long." At first, we stopped at Shields Lake again but the guys coming off the water said there was no bite so we high-tailed it off to German. They also told us the panfish never bite on that lake in the spring until the water temp reaches 62. That day it was 59 on Shields. On German we kept 48 bluegills, two very large perch and a 4-pound pike, all in 4 feet of water. It was a very nice day on the water.

In mid-June of 2020, Doug, Ross and I decided to try some new waters since we still could not get into Canada due to covid restrictions. We checked into a one-bedroom cabin at Sunset Resort on the Ash River Trail which leads into Lakes Kabetogama and Namakan, which are border lakes adjacent to Voyagers National Park. This is a very beautiful and pristine wilderness lake area and we were excited to explore it and fish it hard. To get the boat through the remainder of the Ash River into the lakes we had to pass through a narrows between two tall cliffs which was very cool. On the hot days there were swimmers jumping off the cliff into the deep water.

Our cabin only had one bedroom as a two room was not available. Ross was nice enough to take the couch with his sleeping bag. We had a deck with a charcoal grill. The Ash River Trail has five resorts along its two miles stretch and the boat access was very close by. Just past the last resort there was a store that sold beer, liquor, bait and food. It was the epitome of convenience to pull up to their dock and walked the 60 feet to that store. Our resort also had a gas pump on the dock which we patronized. Premium gas was $2.99 per gallon which we thought was pretty good since we were off the beaten path.

Since this was new water for us, we didn't really know where to start angling. However, after a while, Doug located a productive spot. In 15-18 feet we boated a few walleyes but it was a very rocky area with lots of snags. That day we caught all our fish on Lindy rigs, Dakota harnesses and beaver flickers; jigs would not work.

That evening while frying our fish three boat rigs drove up to the cabin next to us. It was a large cabin that slept 12. The boats were magnificent and large, and we estimated they went for a hundred grand each and were much bigger than my 18-footer. We talked with them every evening. It turned out they were from Oklahoma! They drove all that way to fish smallmouth bass which shocked us. They were not interested in walleyes and fished bass all week. Their goal was to catch 5-pound bass. They casted the shallows all week and caught many in the 4- to 4.5-pound range but never nailed that elusive 5 pounder. While casting the shallows they hooked quite a few big pike in the 10-18-pound range.

These "Okie boys," as we called them, were hilarious. They all had southern accents and used the word "y'all" in pretty much every sentence. They had lots of dirty jokes that kept us laughing all week. When we asked them why they drove so far to catch bass they replied, "to get away from our wives since we can't get a phone signal here!" They had been doing this adventure to that resort for many years. They kept us in stitches all week, although not literally. They called us Yankees.

On our second day we tried Lake Kabetogama. It was breezy so we had a nice walleye chop. Fishing was slow but we came off the lake with five walleyes and two nice sauger. We then elected to fish for big pike in a nearby bay called Blind Bay, which we could not resist due to the name. It was shallow and choked with weeds; prime pike country. Unfortunately, those slimers did not know they were supposed to be there. After casting big stuff for two hours, we boated nothing so we left.

While on the water we actually saw a blue boat full of packages. The word Amazon was emblazoned on its side. We had no idea Amazon had its own delivery boats for remote cabins.

After a steak supper we were relaxing on our deck on that hot day. Two women paddled by us in a canoe and both were topless! We were delighted at their courage and wished we had my binoculars. The guys gave me a detailed description of them for my vicarious benefit. We concluded anything goes on the wild Ash River. One of the Okie boys saw this too and started whistling like a wolf which seemed to motivate the girls to paddle as fast as they could!

The next two days were very hot and fishing was slow. We had to skinny dip twice a day to say comfortable and we dunked our shirts too in order to keep cool. The smallmouth bass fishing this week was the best we ever had. Although we were not fishing for them, they attacked our spinners often. Many were in the 3- to 5-pound range and fought like they were possessed! Sometimes they surface and did cartwheels before shooting away from the boat. Their performance certainly put walleyes to shame. We even kept a few to take home since we hated to go home empty handed.

On our last day of fishing, we finally hit the walleye jackpot on Lake Kabetogama. We found a stretch of water ranging from 12 to 39 feet. We caught quite a few walleyes backtrolling with Lindy rigs and nightcrawlers. This was the only day all week that we got them on crawlers. I boated a 4 pounder and a 5 that afternoon which was our biggest of the week. Another great fish fry was had that night before watching the sunset on our deck.

By the way, we were pleased our cabin had air conditioning. As usual, the guys did all the cooking and I washed all the dishes. Unfortunately, we had a theft at our cabin when we were on the water. Someone stole our bag of charcoal briquets off our deck and a big stick of summer sausage out of our fridge. We did not report it to the resort owner, John.

Just one month later we went back to that same resort for another week of fishing. On the way we drove past a black bear running in the ditch by Washkish as well as a wolf crossing the highway. This time we had a 2-bedroom cabin, and they gave me a room to myself for which I was very grateful. Ross brought 5 pounds of sliced ham and prime steaks, so it was a caveman carnivore week. He also brought a full bar, not to mention 5 pounds of pistachio nuts. Somehow, he was still grumpy all week anyway.

We fished for six days on both Namakan and Kabetogama. Our first day was slow and we actually got lost in a new area. There were dozens of islands and the guys said they all looked alike. Unfortunately, Doug doesn't know how to punch in weigh points on my locator or we would have done so at our dock. After driving around for quite a while they got their bearings. It was a slow day of fishing, but I managed to boat a 5-pound walleye and a 4-pound smallmouth bass. I released them both.

The next day we only caught three walleyes all day but enough for a fish fry that night. Around supper time a nasty thunderstorm rolled in and last until midnight. There was mega lightning lit up like spider webs. We were able to watch it on our deck since the cabin had an overhang.

The next day was Doug's day. He boated seven walleyes and another 18-inch smallie which I kept. We had nice weather and another great fish fry. Crawlers and leeches were the ticket. They were not interested in minnows.

The highlight of the day was when I set the butt of my spinning rod between my thighs in order to grab a sandwich. Before I knew it my rod went over the side of the boat. I lunged for it but missed. I was bummed I lost my favorite Fenwick rod and reel. Only one minute later ross got a snag and reeled it in. Low and behold, it was my wayward rod and reel! Believe it or not, he hooked the last eyelet. I yelled for Doug to grab it before it went back down and he got it just in time and saved it. I told Ross he is my savior and I would gladly kiss his fat butt the rest the day. He muttered something about the rest of his life so I ended up mixing his cocktails the rest of the week which was a Herculean task indeed!

On the morrow, fishing was slow again. We only got four eater walleyes which were enough for supper. Unfortunately, we got caught in a black thunderstorm. The guys eyeballed the shores for a place to pull up off the water since we felt like sitting ducks. There was no such place in sight since the forest came right up to the water's edge. Then we decided to make a run for it back to the resort but the sky looked even worse there. Our only recourse was to get as close to the shore as possible with hopes that a nearby lightning strike would hit the tall tree instead of us. We sat there quite a while before it passed. Luckily, we saw no strikes on land around us. Since the storm wrecked the fishing and it was late afternoon we threw in the towel and boated to our cabin in the rain with serious waves.

They did not feel like cooking, so we drove the mile to the end of the trail in my van to a restaurant named Ash-Namak which was like an animal morgue. There were animal mounts on all the walls including zebra heads, wildebeest, wild boar mounts and of course, deer and moos heads. A couple of them were unrecognizable. Ross and Doug thought it was impressive, but I did not. This café had a skimpy menu; just soups, salads and sandwiches. We all chose steak sandwiches, fries and icy beers. We had a very cute blonde waitress which didn't hurt anything either. However, the service was slow and the food was overpriced, probably to pay for the owners African hunting safaris. After dining we went out onto their stone balcony overlooking the river and feasted our eyes on the scenery while we sucked up another brew.

The next day I got skunked on the water. The highlight of the day was feeding a bald eagle with a dead sauger that did not survive the unhooking. The guys described the spectacular sight in detail. I love feeding those majestic avians. After a good party that night we decided not to ever return to these two lakes. This is smallmouth bass country more so than walleye waters. The cabin rentals were very reasonably priced, however.

In June of 2021, Ken and I checked into Lake Reno resort just outside of Alexandria, Minnesota. Just a couple of miles east of Alex, we saw a sign for Panther Distillery. We did not know there was a distillery there so we thought we better investigate since we were feeling rather touristy. We sampled many types of bourbon for 99 cents each. Our stomachs were empty so it didn't take much. One of the bourbons was very good so I bought a couple of bottles. By the time we got to the resort we were not feeling any pain.

The cabin was adequate and even had a TV, which we did not require. Unfortunately, the docks had boat lifts which were a headache. Somehow Ken cut his hand on it pretty good so I had to doctor him up. When we booked the resort with Dawn, the owner, she was nice as well as honest and confided that Lake Reno, which was the best walleye lake in the area, had a record perch hatch that spring according to the DNR. We knew this would mean poor fishing for walleyes on that water. However, there are 139 lakes in that county of Douglas so we had many choices.

Nevertheless, we decided to start out our first day on Reno. This turned out to be a poor choice. Fishing was terrible and calamity ensued. Ken was in the driver's seat and got a bird's nest in his spinning reel. He pulled out a lot of line which still held his jig and leech. He laid the attached jig on the transom tray which had two drain holes at the back wall. Unbelievably, his jig went down the drain hole without our notice. We started taking on water and the rain got heavier. When we could see standing water under Kens seat, I knew something was wrong. I crawled back there and stuck my arm down to the drain hole. Sure enough his jig was hooked onto the plug and when he pulled on his line the plug came out. I had difficulty unhooking his jig from the plug but finally got it out. The leech was still on the jig and wiggling! I installed the plug and we turned on the bilge pump. The pump could not make much headway due to the torrential rain and I got concerned we might sink since we noticed the back of the boat was riding lower than usual. We decided we better make a run for it so we fired up the 80 horse and headed for shore. Unfortunately, Ken could not find our resort. We were lost and the boat was in danger of sinking! Somehow, I did not start praying out loud.

Like most boaters, Ken made the mistake of not eyeballing our resort when we were leaving the dock so he knew what to look for. He also neglected to punch in the weigh points on my locator so we could follow the way home. He drove around for quite a while and he finally found our docks. We hurriedly hoisted the boat onto the lift for which we were actually grateful. It took a long time but the water drained out completely. We came off the lake with no fish but with our skins intact. Not a good way to start.

On our second day of fishing Roger joined us in my boat. Mike also fished with Bill in his boat on Little Latoka Lake which was deep. Walleye fishing was slow as usual but the weather was dry and windy. Bill boated a 25-inch walleye which he released.

In the afternoon we opted for fillets for supper and pulled out our trusty ultralights for sunfish. We dropped my anchor just three feet from a diving platform and caught one bluegill after another for hours. Most were too little but we kept some bigger ones for supper. There must have been a thousand of them under that dock in eight feet of water. We had a big fish fry in our cabin that evening which fed all five of us.

On Tuesday Ken and I fished alone on Turtle Lake. This was a small, secluded lake not far from our cabin. We sent the whole day there and only saw two other boats. It was so peaceful I did not want to leave. We only caught a few fish, but I boated a 19-inch walleye which we kept for supper. I got my line in the prop so we anchored in shallow water to remove the prop to clear the line. Ken was nice enough to get in the water to do the job. I warned Ken not to drop the cotter pin in the lake but it slipped out of his fingers anyway. Fortunately, I always carry spare cotter pins and wing nuts in my boat. It was a hot day and we were happy to skinny dip. We had a nice fish fry for supper that night with gluten free fish batter which Ken requires. Yuck!

The weed growth in all the area lakes was unusually high for mid-June due to a hot spring. It was more like the growth one expects in mid-August. A perfect example of this was on Big Chippewa Lake. Once again, we had two boats and five anglers. The weeds were emerging in 20 feet of water! We fished that lake hard. Roger gave us a 21-inch walleye to keep, and Ken caught a 23-incher which he released. Mike and I got shut out. We pulled my boat within six feet of the weeds and dropped anchor. We used slip bobbers and jigs but could not coax the fish out of the weeds. We charted few fish that day and concluded most of them were hiding in the tall weeds.

On our last day of fishing, it was just Ken and I again, this time on Lake Mary. Dawn gave us what we thought was a hot tip as someone did well on Mary the day before. We went to the wrong public access and the water was very low. Ken had to get out of the boat and drag it out of the knee-deep water over rocks. As usual, we caught very little. The low light was when I went nuts setting the hook on a fish next to the boat. I shattered my UL rod in three places and had to hand line in a 4-pound pike. We decided that was the last straw so we pounded a beer and left.

We only caught 7 keeper walleyes all week so went home with little. We were not impressed with fishing in the Alexandria area and probably would not return any time soon. Between my snoring and Ken yelling in his sleep in our one-bedroom air-conditioned cabin we went home exhausted. The highlight was fishing six different lakes in six days, as well as the male bonding.

On August 15 of 2021 Ross, Doug and I chose to fulfill a long-standing fishing dream of launch fishing on Lake of the Woods. That morning I took the shuttle to the Mall of America again since we did not need my boat or tackle. The boys picked me up at noon and we had a nice drive to Borderview lodge on Zipple Bay. That night we had supper in the lodge café. The service was slow and the food was overpriced but delicious. We had a nice evening on our deck without any mosquitos, which shocked us.

The next morning the 27-foot launch left at 8 a.m. so we arose early and cooked a he-man breakfast that we hoped would last us all day. Our boat Captain was also named Doug so we figured he would bring us good luck too. We drove out a few miles and dropped our line. We were supplied with baitcasting rods and reels with heavy mono. We were shocked that we were using 3-

ounce sinkers of a type we had never seen before. They were clip on's. He said we had to fish two feet off the bottom so the walleyes could see the nightcrawlers. We used nothing but worms and harnesses with spinners all day.

Captain Doug was very entertaining and talked non-stop the first few hours. He regaled us with countless fishing tales and some ribald jokes. There were six anglers on the boat and we caught lots of saugers and walleyes. Captain Doug caught the biggest, a 28-inch brute. Poor Ross boated baby fish all day but we did not rub it in too much.

That afternoon I had the most exciting and humbling experience of the trip. While trolling forward as usual I hooked something very large. It fought hard for 10 or 15 minutes. My small wrists were getting tired since I never felt anything this heavy before. It stayed down the whole time and when I finally got it right under the boat it made one last mighty downwards plunge. I wasn't prepared for such a powerful jerk and did not have a strong enough grip. The beast jerked the rod out of my hand and I dropped it. When I picked it up the fish was gone! I could not believe I made such a dumb mistake. I am sure it was the biggest walleye of my life; probably a 12-15 pounder! I felt like shit and could not fish for an hour. When I finally got back in the water, I got skunked the rest of the day.

The next day was also hot and windy. We had a different captain who was not as much fun. We caught fish all morning but nothing huge. By early afternoon the wind died and the angling slowed considerably. The captain drove us 20 miles out to Garden Island where we got a few more. Unfortunately, he told us a racist joke which made me very uncomfortable. When I told him it was racist, he did not reply.

The highlight of that day was meeting a woman named Janeen on the boat. She went out on the boat with us without a guy along which was unusual. It turned out that she and her 74-year-old mother were in the cabin next to ours. Since she was so much fun to talk to Doug invited her to join us on our deck after supper. By the way, we came off the water with 30 fish between the six of us anglers. Captain Tyler cleaned our fish.

We cooked our steaks and retired to the deck for a beautiful evening of weather and camaraderie. I was exhausted and after visiting for an hour or so I went to my bunk to rest and read an audiobook. The party finally ended about midnight. For some bizarre reason Ross turned on the TV loud for an hour. I knew Ross long enough to know that if I asked him to turn it down, he would do the opposite so I said nothing.

The next morning came early and we were all a little slow. We rustled up another Paul Bunyan breakfast of flapjacks, maple bacon, and lots of strong black coffee. Ross does his own maple syruping and always brings much of it on our trips. It's the best maple syrup I ever tasted. We said good bye to Janeen and her mother, who had tragic stories, and vowed to keep in touch but we never did.

It was a weird ride home. We drove past two bait shops that were closed and four cafes that were shut down. We were still in the heart of a plague in northern Minnesota and the economy was still not recovered. We finally had to settle on a Subway for late lunch. We got to the mall an hour before the shuttle arrived and the guys were nice enough to wait with me. I boarded it with two Ziploc bags of frozen walleye and sauger fillets. It was another wonderful and successful fishing adventure but, as usual, the biggest one got away. We vowed to return someday. Our guides said October was the best month.

In May of 2022 I went back to the Mississippi river with two guys to fish below the Red Wing dam. It was a disaster! For some reason the boat driver decided to drive the boat south into Lake Pepin instead of north to the dam which is where many walleyes are usually caught. We fished a couple hours and decided to go upriver. The 80-horse motor conked out and we never got it started. I wanted to remove the cowl, but it was too wavy for me to safely stand on the transom tray, so we drove for 30 minutes with my 8-horse motor to find calmer water. It was hard to make headway against the current. When I finally got the hood off the motor the stench of an electrical fire was pungent! The motor head was charred black! We had a fire but we did not see flames since the hood smothered them. We had to drive another hour with the little motor to get to the public access. On the way home we commiserated about how our predicament would have been worse if we only had the one motor. This is precisely why I have two.

When we got my boat to Universal Marine in Rochester, I was told the voltage regulator shorted out and the computer board and manifold were wrecked too. It was hard to round up parts they said it was fixed in June at a cost of $1200. They claimed that motor ran well. As we shall see, that turned out to be untrue.

CHAPTER ELEVEN: THE GRAND FINALES!

In July of 2022 Doug, Ken and I went back to Basket Lake, Ontario, for the first time in 11 years. They finally lifted most of the covid restrictions in Ontario but we still had to jump through some hoops to get across the border. Within 72 hours of crossover, we had to register online that we were coming. We also had to have papers showing that we were vaccinated against covid 19 which we were and we had the papers to prove it. Little did we know it would be both a Murphy's Law trip and the best walleye fishing Ken and I ever had!

Doug and I departed my house in Rochester at 6:30 a.m. with great excitement. We picked up Ken in St. Paul just before 8 and finally headed north. A few miles south of Hinckley we had yet another flat tire on the trailer on the passenger's side, as usual. As we were changing out the flat a very sexy female state trooper stopped to assist us. Her name was Bambi and she had a very sexy voice. We were amazed she was a trooper. The guys said she was gorgeous so she could easily have been a very fine stripper or even Miss Minnesota! She made a point of telling us she is engaged. She was quite friendly and even had a sense of humor which also surprised us. She was certainly the hottest gun-toting woman we ever met! Doug even said he probably wouldn't mind getting arrested by her or even roughed up a little!

Soon we were on the road again and stopped at Slims goodyear Tire Service in Hinckley to buy a new spare tire. I definitely did not want to be stranded in the Canadian wilderness with another flat and no spare. We told Slim about the lady trooper and he said he was in love with her! He confided that he had proposed to her the year before but she turned him down. He also said she is engaged to a big macho stud state trooper who is "built like a brick shithouse." His own words, honest. We laughed and thanked him for the tire which cost $111.

When we finally got to International Falls, we gassed up the van, boat and four gas cans at $4.72 per gallon. We always bring extra gas to Canada since theirs is so expensive. We had no trouble crossing into Ontario and right away noticed their gas was $8!

Just across the bridge over the Rainy River there was a building on one side with a big sign that read CANNABIS, which is now legal in all of Canada. On the other side was a liquor store. We marveled that Canadian entrepreneurs such as they are, finally figured out what American anglers wanted, and we stopped. Doug ran into the cannabis shop to buy some gummies. There was a guy passed out on the floor but the lady behind the bullet proof window was very friendly. In the meanwhile, Ken ran into the liquor shop while I stood next to the boat to guard our belongings.

Very shortly, we were on the road and found a bait shop in Fort Frances. We bought a half flat of crawlers and when I asked the clerk the location of the nearest place to buy eggs, she said they had some for sale. Canada barred us from bringing eggs across the borders due to a minor avian flu outbreak in the Midwest. We bought two dozen and hit the road again with our new non-resident fishing licenses which now cost $42. US currency!

We headed our rig north on the 502 to Dryden. We drove past a boat, motor and trailer upside down in a deep ravine and there was an official looking truck stopped to help. We were relieved there were no ambulances around. In Dryden we stopped at Walmart to get a rainsuit for Ken since his was shabby. They had no rainsuits or even a poncho. We then turned onto the trans-Canadian highway for 35 miles to our turnoff. This gravel road was worse than we remembered; a true washboard. Our top speed was 20 mph. When we got to the little bridge over a stream, we stopped to pee over the side into the river which we did every time in the past. It was a sentimental and silly tradition which somehow made us even happier all over again. It also meant we were nearly at the lodge so the excitement was building after the lengthy journey.

It seemed like the 14-mile trek on that gravel road would never end. When we finally arrived, the office was vacant. We found the resort operator down by the water and Loren admitted us to cabin 8 which he said was an upgrade due to a cancellation. It was a large 2-bedroom cabin with a big living room that contained a sofa bed. Ever the gracious one, Ken volunteered to take that bed. Loren also told us only three of eight cabins were in use that week! This meant we would practically have the resort and the lake to ourselves! Yippeee! We unloaded our gear and fried burgers for a late supper with nightcaps. We were revved up but tired at the same time since it was nearly a twelve hour ride that day.

The next morning, we had bacon and eggs for breakfast. We were shocked that every egg was numbered up to nine digits! Apparently, the Canadians, always overprotective, had numbered and tracked every egg laid in their gigantic province of Ontario! We could not believe it. Their eggs tasted as good as ours though. It helped that both Ken and Doug were good cooks. I washed all the dishes that week.

That day Murphy's Law reared its ugly head once again. Doug is the best boat handler I ever fished with but when he backed my boat down the narrow concrete ramp the port trailer wheel went off the side. The trailer axle was resting on concrete! My van could not pull the boat back up the ramp since the van rode so low. We begged the guy in the next cabin to help us. He hooked the trailer to his big truck and pulled it up. The sound of the trailer dragging on concrete was horrible and made me cringe. I feared my trailer was wrecked. However, we finally got the boat in the water and we even remembered to put in the drain plug.

Unfortunately, neither motor would start. After about 20 minutes Doug fired up the 80 horse but it would not stay running. We then noticed that the T in the gas lines was broken and dripping gasoline! We could not get enough pressure in either line to run the motors. Finally, Loren tried it but to no avail. He got us a 2-gallon gas can that was full and attached to a gas line. We could not connect the hose to the big motor, but it fit the socket on the 8-horse trolling motor.

It turned out that we had to fish with our little trolling motor all week. Among other things, this meant we could not get to the best fishing spot on the lake since it was eight miles at the far end of Basket Lake. It also meant we would not be fishing the magical Little Basket Lake which was nearly as far. Furthermore, since the 18-gallon gas tank built into the boat was full it really slowed us down. Our maximum speed was a pitiful 5.8 mph! We were bummed out and figured we probably would not catch much all week. Wrong.

Our first morning on the water was intermittent drizzle. We drove out a mile from the dock and found a weed patch. We fished that all day and boated 20 walleyes which was a pleasant surprise. They were hitting on jigs and leeches which was great since we loved jigging. I used a jig without a body but a small Indiana blade attached to the head. That night we had our first fish fry. Why is it that fresh walleyes in Canada seem to taste even better than Minnesota ones? I brought my little pocket voice recorder with me and at the end of each night made a recording of the day's events with each guy chipping in their two cents worth. Much laughter was had by all. One reason I did this is to relish the fond memories during our long winter when we were yearning to get back on the water for which we had to wait so long.

The next day we hit the walleye jackpot! Loren told us that morning about a rock reef about a mile from camp which held fish. We managed to find it in 10-12 feet of water. Ken went nuts that morning and probably boated twenty walleyes himself including a pair of 24 inchers. That afternoon under heavy clouds but no rain I boated a 28-inch 8-pound walleye, the biggest of my life! We took photos of me holding up the hog and released it alive. Almost all the walleyes we caught that week were fat and looked very healthy with nice coloring. No sickly ones like we sometimes get in our home state. Since I caught the biggest one, I had naming rights. Since this spot pretty much salvaged our trip, I chose the name of Resurrection Rocks!

Doug could not catch a 20 incher for a long time but got silly on his first gummy. Later in that afternoon when it was not raining there was a very loud clap of thunder right above us. I yelled, "hit the deck" and dropped to my knees. We had to get off the lake but there was no place to pull up since the trees came right up to the water's edge. We spotted a very large beaver lodge nearby that looked new so pulled up on it. The guys said it was probably 50 feet in diameter; certainly the biggest one we ever saw. It was comprised of rock, mud and many sticks and branches. We marveled at how sturdy it was.

We stood in the drizzle sipping bourbon for 45 minutes until the storm finally passed. We never saw any beavers for which we were grateful. We caught a few more walleyes before heading to shore for fish cleaning and supper. That day we boated 80 walleyes which we counted; our most ever anywhere! Ken fired up his tabletop gas grill and made giant pork chops for supper. A fine time was had by all but we were sick of rain.

The next day, Tuesday, it was raining again but we were happy to start out with a breakfast fish fry with toast and lots of coffee. The fishing was very good on Resurrection Rocks in the morning but slowed in the afternoon so we putted out to that weed patch we discovered on our first day on the water. We caught a few more. By 3:30 the rain really picked up so I suggested we head into our cabin for happy hour and an early supper. They agreed. We said we would come back out if the rain let up after eating and cleaning up the kitchen. Ken grilled big steaks for us with beer and instant mashed potatoes which was very satisfying.

At 6:30 we were back on the water but fishing was dead. Then the rain began all over again in a steady pattern. After an hour we had enough and chose to quit for the day. Considering the weather, we felt we did quite well catching 31 more walleyes. As we were about to depart Ken noticed a giant colorful rainbow across the lake. Each end of it went into the water. Just then a huge bald eagle flew directly into that rainbow. Ken said it was breath taking. One of the reasons we go to Canada is to experience this level of phenomenal natural beauty which is so bountiful in my second favorite country.

On Wednesday we finally had warm sunshine! No more rainsuits. We had put out our marker buoy on Resurrection Rocks but it was gone that morning. Somehow Ken managed to rig up one for us using an empty orange juice bottle, some rope and a rock we caught off the bottom of the lake. It actually held and we had a good day on the water. Doug got tired of trolling so we dropped my anchor and slip bobbered. We nailed them that way too and ended up catching 59 walleyes this day.

Unfortunately, we had a fish bite accident in the boat. Doug was hammering the big walleyes that morning and caught 24 fish over 20 inches! While trying to unhook a 25 incher he dropped the fish and its teeth gouged a hole on the inside of his wrist on the way down. He said he could actually see his vein! I got out

the first aid kit and he finally got the bleeding stopped.
Although we disinfected it every night with hydrogen peroxide it
still got infected since he did not cover up the clean wound. He
did not know he was supposed to do so.

Weather-wise, the next day was an unusual day on the lake.
Warm sun all day without a breath of wind. For some reason we
did not understand, there were no waterfowl or any birds
around us all day. It was total silence all day and very peaceful
but a bit eerie. Another idyllic day on the beautiful water which
was not gin clear which really helped the fishing on such a clear
day.

On Thursday we chose to buy some minnows at the resort for
$7. Per dozen. They were nice sized and the walleyes could not
leave them alone. It was pretty much instant bite every time we
dropped our jigs in the water. We went through three dozen in
just three hours and then went back to leeches and some
worms. While jigging with my last minnow I hooked a big fish.
After a tussle of five minutes, it finally surfaced, and Doug
netted it for me. It was another hog! After weighing it, and
measuring, it was the exact same size as the one I caught two
days earlier: 28 inches and 8 pounds! After more photos Doug
insisted that I boated the same fish twice that week. We never
could prove it either way but managed to release it alive.

We decided to cast for pike that hot afternoon so we headed
for a large weed patch. We had fun boating some of those
slimers and it was a true gator bowl as we each tried to top the
other in size. Ken and Doug each boated a 36 incher but Kens
was fatter. No big ones today. After a while we went back to

Resurrection Rocks for more walleyes but they were not very active. Nevertheless, we boated 41 of that species on this day.

We cleaned some more walleyes and grilled big cheeseburgers for supper with canned veggies. Our cabin did not have a microwave. None of them do since they were too taxing on the big electrical generator in the woods. We were totally cut off from civilization for seven days. I brought a table radio but could not pick up a single station on AM or FM. There was no TV and our phones did not get a signal all week. We loved this and it was a great getaway. We did not miss the news at all.

On our last day of fishing, it was hot and sunny again. We chose not to skinny dip due to so many pike who have needle sharp teeth. Instead, we dunked our shirts in the lake and wrung them out then put them back on to cool our skin which was very soothing. We spent the morning on Resurrection Rocks again after buying four dozen more minnows. We caught 42 walleyes that morning and Doug had bragging rights with a 26 incher.

In the afternoon sun we drove back to the weed patch for more pike fishing. I hooked something very big and it headed straight ahead of the boat. It took out most of my line. I kept yelling to Doug to drive forward but he would not do it. He was afraid my line would end up in the prop. My 12-pound test line finally broke just before all the line was stripped off my spool. I couldn't help but curse him which he was used to since we knew each other for forty years. Doug had the biggest pike of the day; a 38 incher that was probably about 16 pounds. They boated many that day.

That night we had our last celebratory walleye fry for supper and really gorged ourselves since they were so fresh. They went great with Bush's baked beans. We pulled the boat out that night with Loren's help in his truck since we wanted to make an early departure the next day. When we went to the office that Saturday morning to settle up, we noticed there was no payment device on the counter. We were supposed to pay in cash or checks but did not know this. We had no checks and not enough cash. Loren gave us the resort address on paper and said he would hold our cabin reservation for July of 2023 if he received our checks. We mailed them out the next week and he eventually cashed them.

I was disappointed that the resort owner, Dr. Anita, who is so special, was not around all week. Loren said she was touring Argentina that week. We said farewell and had an uneventful drive to the border. We got across without getting searched and had a feast at McDonalds in International Falls at noon. It was crowded. While in the restaurant a goose crapped in my boat which the guys were nice enough to clean out for me.

About 20 miles north of my former hometown of Cloquet we had yet another flat tire! This time it was on the driver's side of the trailer for a change. Unfortunately, there was no shoulder, so it was scary to squat down with cars flying by just three feet away. They did not let me get out of the van since they were afraid I would wander into traffic and get killed. We stopped in Cloquet at L & M supply to buy another new spare tire which only cost $66.

Doug and I got to my house in Rochester and ordered a pizza at 10 pm. We tallied up our fish for the week: 273 walleyes and 52 northern pike! We each came home with a limit of four walleyes and Ken and I had limits of four pike each which Doug always hated cleaning. We cleaned so many fish we dulled all four of our fillet knives and I neglected to bring my electric sharpener. A nice problem to have.

By the way, for the first time ever I brought wine to Canada instead of beer. Somehow that just didn't work. Hard to beat an icy beer on a hot day so won't bring wine again although we had no trouble polishing off the entire 5-liter tapper box of chardonnay which went well with fish.

A few days later a friend helped me get my boat to Al's Specialty marine in Rochester. They found four things wrong with my 80-horse motor that the previous marine shop missed. Al's fixed everything. They also discovered that the trailer axle was bent which was causing many flat tires in the past ten years. We replaced that axle too and had no more flats since. I decided to stick with Al's from now on.

It was another fantastic and even heavenly fishing trip that spoiled us as always. It was always sad to put CLOUD 9 in winter storage that fall.

What follows is the only fish story in this book that does not involve me, but I had to include it since it was pretty crazy. On June 4, 2023, while sitting at the local rock and roll church, the harmonicist in the band sat with me a while for a visit. He told me he was fishing a local gravel pit lately in his electric boat. He had his 6-pound Yorkshire terrier in the boat too. Steve hooked a big fish on a rooster tail jig. When he finally got it to the surface it was a two-foot walleye! The dog went nuts, jumped in the water, and bit the walleye! Steve managed to net both at the same time! Fortunately, he did not fillet either one!

Finally, Ross, Doug and I went back to Basket Lake, Ontario in July of 2023. We left my house at 7, after a breakfast of leftover Godfather's pizza and coffee. We cruised without incident to Cloquet where we gassed up the boat, van and five cans, two of which had those new-fangled spouts which are terrible. Cloquet usually has the cheapest gas in the northland so we spent over $200. At BP for $3.18 per gallon. Then we stopped at Outdoor Advantage baits in Cloquet. We bought 1.5 pounds of mixed leeches. They were small but very cute. LOL

We topped off at International Falls and bought eggs since we were now allowed to bring them across the border. We got through quickly and without incident. We had to pay $11. To use the bridge across the Rainy River. That bridge is owned by the Boise Cascade paper mill which is adjacent. We stopped at rainy River Baits in Fort Francis to buy 250 crawlers and licenses. When we got across there was a cannabis shop on the right. Ross and Doug went in to purchase THC which I don't use. Doug bought some gummies and Ross bought some smokeable stuff that smelled just like a skunk. Yuck!

Then we drove to the 502 across the long bridge. This highway is smooth but so curvy you can't pass hardly anywhere. When we finally arrived in Dryden, Ontario the excitement was mounting. The last 14 miles was terrible wash board gravel. Twice we drove across little streams covering the road and then across a complete washout area.

When we finally arrived, we checked in with Loren, the operator, who said Dr. Anita, the owner, was in Iceland. He assigned us to cabin 8 which we reserved a year ahead. It was a 2-bedroom trailer with a deck. When we got to our cabin, we discovered it was occupied! We told Loren who knocked on the door but no answer. There were belongings on the deck and inside. Loren over booked that cabin. We were getting very concerned that we might have to go back home when he said we could take cabin 5. This was a 3 bedroom which he gave us for the price of the 2 bedroom since it was his mistake. We were relieved and it turned out that this was a better place to stay anyway. We had hot showers, but the tap water cannot be consumed, so said the little sign. We always cart in our own drinking water.

We unloaded our gear and had a late supper of cheeseburgers. The water level was down 1.5 feet so Ross and Doug had difficulty launching my boat since the water at the end of the cruddy ramp was only a foot deep. However, since they are farm boys used to maneuvering heavy equipment, I knew they would get the job done and they did.

The next morning, we started out on Resurrection rocks again, but the walleyes were not there like last year. Due to bad weather, we did not want to venture out to the far end of the lake to a better fishing spot, so we did not catch a lot that day.

Monday morning, we cruised out to gull rock flats and caught lots of walleyes before the winds came up. Then we sheltered in a small bay. Then the rains came. It was a downpour, so we were living in our rainsuits again. Even when it let up, we hardly caught anything in that bay, but it was beautiful as was the rainbow late that afternoon. We caught enough walleyes to have our first fish fry that night which was delicious.

This summer there were a lot of forest fires across Canada and often the smoke permeated most of Minnesota. We were concerned it might be smoky at our resort, so I brought masks just in case. We lucked out as there was no smoke all week. The nearby fires by Sioux Lookout got rained out a week earlier so our air was fresh and smelled clean all week. We were grateful and relieved.

On Wednesday we had our best day of fishing in 20-25 feet of water. We finally bought resort minnows at $8. Per dozen. This made all the difference as we boated 66 walleyes, most in the 19–24-inch range on jigs and floaters.

On Thursday the fishing was slow and we only got 31 fish. The highlight for me and only me was that I decided to have a little party in the boat late that afternoon. I drank a few ounces of bourbon in the boat and ended up singing "Over the Rainbow" all over again several times. Afterwards the guys told me I was the worst singer in the world! We chortled. At least I didn't do any cartwheels in the boat!

Friday was our last day and we ended up catching 57 walleyes. However, late afternoon some black clouds closed in from both sides of us so we got off the water. We stood in the fish cleaning house for 45 minutes, concerned about lightning which we never did witness. Doug took a photo of me standing on shore with a double rainbow in the background which is posted at the end of this book. Disregard the stogie.

We had to vacate the cabin that Saturday by 7:30 so had no time to cook breakfast. I had a cold, leftover burger and coffee. Unfortunately, my van would not start: dead battery. Loren gave us a jump with his truck and my cables, and we never turned off the motor all day. Loren charged us for 14 dozen minnows even though we only bought ten.

When we were cruising south on the 502, we actually saw a man lying on the shoulder of the highway with a dog by his side. The guy had his arm in the air and thumb extended. He was hitch hiking lying down! We had never seen this before and wondered if it was a Canadian tradition of some sort. He was literally in the middle of nowhere but wilderness with no turnoffs in the area. We speculated on how he got there: either dumped off or walked for many miles. We were afraid to pick him up.

Fort Francis was jammed with boat traffic and we waited in line for 30 minutes to get across the border. We got lunch to go at McDonalds in International Falls. We managed to get all the way to Cloquet before gassing up again. It was an uneventful journey home and, for once, we did not even have a flat tire!

Both outboard motors and the locator worked perfectly all week.

We did not do any slip bobbering and simply back trolled all week which Doug loved. He drove the boat all week. Our total fish count for the week was 239 walleyes with a few dozen pike.

Our biggest walleye was only 25.5 inches and biggest pike was only 32 inches. Both caught by Doug, sad to say. We came home with our limit of four little walleyes. We reserved a cabin for 2024. We wanted cabin 5 again but Loren had just promised it to others, so we settled for 8 again. We got to my house in Rochester at 6:30 and Ross drove home while Doug spent the night. We took turns napping on the 11-hour ride home.

Now my story is almost over for the time being. However, since I am only 71 years old, I expect to be on the water many more years. Canada here we come!

EPILOGUE

We were fishing Basket Lake, Ontario once again. We were in the deepest part of the lake when I hooked a bad snag. It was so solid I guessed it was a boulder. We backed up so I could get on the other side. Suddenly, the snag moved perpendicular from the boat slowly! It had to be a fish. I never felt anything like this before. I held on as best I could, grateful I had heavy line on a heavy action rod. I could not make any headway even with the motor off. It started pulling the boat around in a big circle, slowly! After about an hour of exhausting labor we finally made some headway on the brute. When it finally surfaced, we could not believe our eyes. It was about 9 feet long! There was no way to get it in my 18-foot boat, so we dragged it to shore which was not easy. When we got it on the sandy beach we jumped out of the boat and dragged it up on the sand a couple more feet. We stood there aghast, wondering what it was. We did not recognize this leviathan which looked ancient.

I had the strangest urge to touch its head so I laid my hands on its forehead. Somehow, I could hear it communicating with me telepathically! It said it was a thousand years old and its name was Gumtoh. It said it was the last of its species on Earth. It asked me to save its life. I said I would and told it I love it.

The three of us guys pushed it back into the water where it wallowed away from the beach. It then dove to the dark depths, never to be seen again by human eyes.

Then I woke up, damn it! I have had this same dream many times in my adult life. I have now lost nearly all of my eyesight. I only have light perception left. I have kept my promise to myself to keep on living my dreams despite my blindness. I shall continue to do so, although it is very challenging, more than anyone knows. To do otherwise would involve sacrificing some of my hard-earned self-respect which I shall never surrender. I have instructed Doug that when I die it is in my will that I will be cremated. I told him he must pour my ashes in Lake Woebegone and he said he would!

As I write this book, I often felt like I was re-living each episode. It made me realize just how much fun I have had in my fishing therapy. It also made me realize how much adversity we had, as in life itself.

Thank you all for taking this wonderful journey with me. I hope you enjoyed it as much as I loved sharing it with you.

Finally, from the bottom of my heart, I wish to thank all my fishing soul mates for patiently enabling me to fulfill this exciting portion of my self-promise and my dream. I love you for it and always will. You assisted me every step of the way on every fishing excursion for decades. Only very fine men would do this for that long. You should get medals for your kindness despite all the practical jokes you played on me! LOL

"In spite of ourselves, we'll end up sitting on a rainbow"

-John Prine

THE END

Made in the USA
Monee, IL
12 August 2023

40912442R00115